D'You Remember Yer Man?

D'You Remember Yer Man?

A Portrait of Dublin's Famous Characters

BOBBY AHERNE

NEW ISLAND

D'YOU REMEMBER YER MAN?
First published in 2014
by New Island Books
16 Priory Hall Office Park
Stillorgan
County Dublin
Republic of Ireland

www.newisland.ie

Text Copyright © Bobby Aherne, 2014
Images Copyright © Ruan van Vliet, 2014

Bobby Aherne and Ruan van Vliet have asserted their moral rights.

PRINT ISBN: 978-1-84840-377-2
EPUB ISBN: 978-1-84840-378-9
MOBI ISBN: 978-1-84840-379-6

British Library Cataloguing Data. A CIP catalogue record for this book is available from the British Library

Typeset by JVR Creative India
Cover design by Ruan van Vliet
Printed by ScandBook AB, Sweden

10 9 8 7 6 5 4 3 2 1

Contents

Dedicated to anybody who has ever made their city a more interesting place to be.

Foreword: C'mere Till
I Tell Ya

To most people in this world, a 'character' is – by definition – a fictional being who appears in a novel, movie, cartoon, play or video game. But in a windswept little town on the east coast of a small island on the third rock from the sun, that noun has been used for years to refer to walking, talking, real-life citizens who are often even more fantastical and far-fetched than those made up by creative writers. In the arts, a character is a device designed to lead the reader or viewer through a story, helping them to understand the plot, decipher the themes and empathise with different perspectives. This is no different in the real world, where a study of the eccentric and renowned characters of Dublin allows us to trace the *real* history of the city. In this book, through a hundred or so individual portraits, we can observe the mindset of Dubliners over the past 400 years, through their personalities, their attitudes and – perhaps most importantly – their sense of humour and irreverence.

The art critic William Hazlitt once said that 'a nickname is the heaviest stone that the devil can throw at a man,' but we can safely assume that he had never been to Dublin, where – in most cases – a nickname can be worn like a badge of honour – an affectionate stone, perhaps, thrown at certain people by their neighbours and cohabitants. In fact, many of the new friends that you are about to meet possess ludicrous pseudonyms. Just look at the likes of Bang Bang, Fortycoats, or even Mad Mary – all of whom are local legends remembered with great fondness. That said, I once heard about a man who mentioned to his friends that he'd love to have a cool nickname – but expressing this desire was such a social faux pas that from that day forth, he was simply known as 'Duckshite'. So I suppose that some nicknames are indeed better than others. Some other people who might agree with Mr Hazlitt's theory include Hot Potato (a man with a head like a red hot potato, who would chase anyone who shouted 'Hot Potato' at him), Clappy (he'd chase you if you clapped at him), Wagon Wheels (he'd chase anyone who shouted 'Wagon Wheels' at him) and Rusty Razors (you're probably getting the hang of this by now). It seems like in the olden days, before the arrival of technology, there was nothing more enjoyable for a young Dubliner to do than provoking a good chase from a furious grown-up.

Some of our characters were so-called 'knights of the road' with no fixed abode, whose way of life might inspire pity. But they usually seemed so content in their ways that they bring to mind the meeting of Alexander the Great and Diogenes, when the king approached the resting beggar and asked him if there were anything that he could do for him. The poor man simply replied 'Yes... stand out of my light.' Like Diogenes, most of our motley crew seemed to have had it all sussed – although there are also a few poor unfortunates from the twentieth century who went off to war as fit young men and returned home, shell-shocked, to a place where they no longer fitted in.

As is the nature of folklore, stories change rapidly as they are passed from one person to another – a lesson that we learned early on in life through schoolyard games like 'Chinese Whispers' or 'Telephone'. In modern-day Dublin, there's a middle-aged fellow who seems to spend every day sitting outside coffee shops jotting in a notepad, dressed in a Hawaiian shirt, a garish gilet and a big fur-lined trapper hat. I once mentioned his existence to a friend and was told – very matter-of-factly – that this man had made enough money from the stock markets to afford this coffee-guzzling, people-watching, poetry-writing, *flâneur* lifestyle. Then somebody else told me that he had actually inherited lots of properties and was living off the rent from them. Another in-the-know observer claimed that he had made enough money as an architect to enable an early retirement. Finally, my uncle had heard that this fellow had authored a hugely successful children's book and now lives off his royalty cheques.

At least my uncle's preposterous theory can be eliminated from the equation, as everybody knows that there's no money in publishing.

Regardless of the truth, by living an unusual lifestyle and by dressing in an unorthodox fashion, this fellow has essentially placed himself within the public domain, where his mysterious life story is up for debate and subject to gossip and rumour. Make no bones about it – this book is the product of some extreme people-watching down through the years. The fact is that people are nosey, Dublin is tiny, and its people tend to talk a whole load of shite.

Shades of primitive celebrity culture surround all of our local characters – some more so than others. One eccentric gentleman by the name of Brendan Kilkenny is always certain to turn heads around town for his waist-length, peroxide blonde mullet and dazzling array of sports jackets, shirts and ties. My brother and I have very fond memories of listening to his bizarre pirate radio show *The Loveline* in the 1990s, where he signed off each episode with the immortal catchphrase 'keep on smoochin.' In 2002, he entered the major leagues when he briefly decamped to London and auditioned for every talent competition on television – much to the chagrin of the judges. His claim that he was 'Ireland's number one entertainer' was backed up by some truly astonishing scissor kicks and a tone-deaf karaoke-style rendition of 1976 Eurovision winner 'Save All Your Kisses For Me'. He's also famed for running singles nights, offering escort services, and for receiving a truly revolting pedicure on the British reality TV show *The Salon*. It's always a delight to spot the irrepressible Mr Kilkenny in the city, still kicking – in every sense of the word.

Another character of my time was a Blanchardstown native who was never spotted without a flagon of cider in his hands, which led to him being known as 'Two Litre Peter'. Since his passing, Two Litre Peter has been immortalised with a plaque outside of the local barbershop. Unfortunately, not all of our characters are lucky enough to be remembered in such a way – although one fittingly peculiar monument can be seen in The Coombe, where the names of a few random characters (including Johnny Wet Bread, The Lady Hogan and The Magic Soap Man) are engraved onto the steps of the portico to the old maternity hospital; the rest of the building was demolished in 1967. Fortycoats, Hairy Lemon and Bang Bang also get a mention in 'The Mero' by folk balladeer Pete St. John, a fellow better known for songs like 'The Fields of Athenry' and 'Rare Oul Times'. 'The Sick Bed Of Cuchulainn' by The Pogues even gives a little nod to Billy in the Bowl – although it's arguable whether Billy is deserving of any tributes, based on what is known about him. Apart from these few allusions, our street characters have largely been remembered in the oral tradition.

Several years ago, I decided that I wanted to read something about all of these Dubliners – the renegades, the dreamers, the outsiders, the entertainers and the madmen… the people who do whatever they feel like and don't give a damn about what anybody else thinks. 'That would make for a great book,' I thought to myself, possibly aloud. Alas, no library, bookshop or website stocked such a volume, and so I took it upon myself to bring one into existence. According to Dublin oracle Éamonn Mac Thomáis, you'd often see the likes of Bang Bang, Shellshock Joe, All Parcels, Houdini and Hairy Yank cosying up next to each other along the hot wall of Thompson's Bakery on Bridgefoot Street. But apart from that bakery wall, this 'buke' represents the first time that such a crowd of them have been brought together at once. Their stories are often hilarious, sometimes tragic, but always fascinating. These are the wonderful people who Dubliners remember best – the ones who elicit nostalgia, the ones who spark up conversation, the ones who induce smiles and laughs, and the ones responsible for a countless number of individuals turning to each other, smiling and saying 'Ah, d'you remember yer man?'

Aidan Walsh

Aidan Walsh, the self-proclaimed 'Master of the Universe,' was born in 1954 and attended Cork's Lota School for Boys, which he ultimately ran away from to follow his dream of becoming – in his words – 'the head guy over the army.' Walsh never received his promotion. After marching in a few military parades, he complained of sore feet and was discharged in 1972.

He arrived in Dublin not long before the entirety of Temple Bar was due to be razed in order to make way for a new bus terminal. In the meantime, the decrepit buildings were being rented out for next to nothing, encouraging an influx of artists and musicians to the area. Aidan and his pal Paddy Dunning took advantage of the cheap rates being offered and founded Temple Lane Recording Studios and Rehearsal Rooms. While Dunning was the more level-headed of the pair, Walsh saw the project as an opportunity to try to net himself £100,000, which he claimed was the going rate for a German inventor's groundbreaking latest invention – a metal suit that would enable to wearer to live for a million years. According to its creator, the allocated time would start ticking as soon as the user had activated the costume's elixir-like properties… by filling it up with their own urine. As the music studio transpired to be a great success, we can only assume that Aidan got his suit and will be around to celebrate the coming of another thousand millennia. Interestingly, the activities of Dunning, Walsh and their contemporaries actually inspired Dublin City Council; as a result of all the young, creative types infesting the area, the planned bus station was scrapped and Temple Bar was officially designated 'Dublin's Cultural Quarter.'

Walsh later set up a video production company. Callers to the advertised phone number got through to a busy Temple Bar pub, which Aidan used as his headquarters. Despite this slightly unprofessional touch, he managed to get hired to document a high society wedding – the union of a barrister and a solicitor. But his film-making career came to an abrupt end after he recorded the entire day's proceedings and then realised that he'd forgotten to insert the tape.

In 1987, he signed Ireland's fastest ever record deal, thanks to his truly unique rendition of 'The Hokey Cokey'. His debut album *A Life Story of My Life* was a minor hit, with songs such as 'Kissin' and Eatin' with Women', 'I'm the World's Greatest Bankrobber' and 'Laughing My Way Out of the Army'. Around this time, it became common to see Walsh dressed in a gold suit with a cape wrapped around him and a turban on his head, riding a white horse around town.

He drew up plans to have a building on Aston Quay turned into a 'Rock 'n' Roll Hotel', with a direct underground link to Dublin Airport to grant A-list celebrities a paparazzi-free journey to and from the city. For the safety of his clientele, he also proposed a nuclear shelter to be built in front of the hotel, under the River Liffey. His ludicrous, impossible bid of £3,000,000 for the premises led to an actual bidding war with one of the world's richest and most powerful men. Richard Branson, however, had no idea that he was competing against Aidan Walsh, so he kept offering more money. As you can imagine, it wasn't long before the latest branch of Virgin Megastore was opening on Walsh's dream site. On the first day of business, a disgusted Walsh, on horseback, led a procession of his fans, wearing luminous buckets on their heads, along the quays and into the shop. His stallion then emptied its bowels all over the freshly-carpeted music store. Branson's shop went out of business in 2002; 'The Rock 'n' Roll Hotel' remains to be built.

In 1997, Walsh ran for election to the Dáil. Alas, he came in with just 0.12% of the public vote, losing out to one Bertie Ahern. Although he may not have been democratically elected as leader of Ireland, he is still universally recognised as the Master of the Universe.

Aidan Walsh

All Parcels

Back in the day, waste paper had a value around Dublin that today's unemployed recyclers could only dream about. A decent sackful of expired newspapers was worth a few coppers down at the lumberyard, which would help keep you in tea and bread for another day. At a time when jobs and money were as scarce as each other, collecting paper proved to be the only source of income for some of the city's poorest citizens. Things got even more competitive when youngsters joined in, trying to cobble together enough money for a Saturday afternoon double bill down at one of the local picture-houses.

Unable to imagine a luxury such as the cinema was one old beggar woman, whose reliance on this way of life meant that people referred to her as 'All Parcels'. In the 1930s, it was a familiar sight to see her traipsing around Thomas Street and James's Street all day every day, gathering up every last scrap of paper she spotted. What was even more unique about her was the fact that, rather than carelessly tossing everything into a big bag, she'd delicately fold her harvest into neat little parcels, which she tucked under her arms to facilitate their transportation.

A lot of the locals felt great pity for All Parcels, but this pity was always accompanied by a pang of admiration for the fact that a desperate soul like her could fulfil her tedious daily duties with such panache.

All Parcels

Annie Fruitcake

I wish I were able to tell you that Annie Fruitcake earned her pseudonym because she was a fantastic baker who loved to give free samples of her wares to all of her neighbours. Alas, there is no evidence to suggest that she was a confectioner of any sort. Her name derived from the dual facts that she was christened 'Annie' by her parents and that she was as nutty as a fruitcake.

She used to sit on a rock all day, asking passers-by where they lived and threatening to slit the throats of those privileged enough to live in a private house. The children who lived in the tenements could pass by her outpost without fearing for their lives, but the posh kids would make sure that they steered well clear of Annie Fruitcake and her curious ideals.

The Bah Man

The Bah Man was a sickly looking man in his thirties who sat on O'Connell Street sketching his surroundings all day, with his shiny red nose sticking out from beneath his peaked cap. In the evening, with all of his self-imposed artistic duties fulfilled for the day, he'd stroll up and down our main street hunting for prey.

As soon as he spotted a few girls walking along together, he leapt out in front of them, flung his hands in the air and screamed the word 'BAH!' into their faces with terrifying volume. Usually a word lifelessly uttered in a blasé fashion to denote boredom or disinterest, The Bah Man can certainly be credited with breathing a new lease of life into the expression.

Not that this vocabular reinvention ever impressed the girls whose paths he had crossed – they'd have to take a moment to post-traumatically collect themselves before continuing along their way. Laughing away delightedly, The Bah Man continued on his quest to scope out his next unwitting victims.

Bang Bang

During the 1950s and 1960s, a bedraggled man by the name of Thomas Dudley would regularly jump on-board the back of a bus, point his weapon at the driver's head, bark at him to 'keep driving', and then open fire at fellow passengers and passing pedestrians. He sometimes spiced things up for his own amusement, playing a macabre little game where the goal was to shoot everyone on the lower deck before the conductor even had a chance to call for fares.

How did such a ruthless and cold-blooded killer manage to evade the law for so long? Well, it helped that this was Bang Bang: one of the most adored personalities in Dublin, and a man who used a huge brass key instead of a gun. Some people claimed that this key opened the door to a local church, but Bang Bang maintained that it came all the way 'from Germany, from Hitler himself.'

It was commonplace for Dudley's victims to shoot back at him. Commuters would use their umbrellas as rifles, whilst the bus conductor took aim with his ticket machine. And as the bus rolled down O'Connell Street, guards on the beat – noticing the ensuing carnage – got down on their knees, steadied their shots, and targeted Bang Bang through the imaginary crosshairs of their batons. Bedlam ensued, as rush hour Dublin turned into a full-blown battlefield.

Born in April 1906, Dudley was raised in an orphanage in Cabra. He became obsessed with cowboy films as a child, just around the time that Dublin's first picture houses were opening their doors. This was when we were given The Metropole, The Tivoli, The Ambassador, The

Pillar and The Corinthian (which was even dubbed 'The Ranch' due to the amount of Westerns they screened). When John Wayne – born the year after our hero – became the iconic figurehead of the genre, Dudley had found his role model. And when our own Lone Ranger first laid his hands on that mysterious oversized key, he had found his six-shooter.

It wasn't long before Dubliners knew to keep their eyes peeled for Bang Bang as they went about their day, knowing that he could appear at any moment, brandishing his 'firearm' and slapping his rear end as if he were on horseback.

Bang! Bang! You're shot. If yeh don't die, I'm not playin!'

People would happily drop everything to join in the game. Postmen rummaged through their sacks, hoping to find a parcel big and strong enough to act as a shield. Bank clerks on lunch breaks feigned wounds and slumped to the ground around College Green. Guinness workers stopped loading barrels onto their horse and cart, and took cover behind them instead. One Marlborough Street shoot-out lasted a whole half hour, after a gang of American tourists overcame their initial bewilderment and started retaliating.

The inner-city kids always put up a fight, ambushing Bang Bang in packs. Still, they were no match for that loaded key, and it wouldn't be long before the usually lively streets of Blackpitts were piled high with slain baddies, and Dudley emerged victorious to die another day. He even had a habit of appearing at the cinema, guns blazing, during the most dramatic scene in the movie. The packed theatre would be watching a tense standoff, or sitting with bated breath as the sheriff made his ultimate arrest, when suddenly Bang Bang would storm in and turn the place into a bloodbath.

Some people noticed patterns in his behaviour. If you shot him outside The Metropole on O'Connell Street, he'd shout 'Ya missed me!' But if you got him by The Corinthian on Eden Quay, he'd fall to the ground and roll down to the curb, fatally wounded (although, moments later, he'd jump up and swing onto the back of the next bus headed up towards Summerhill). He once fell off a bus during a particularly nasty gunfight. People gathered round to see if he was hurt, but he just brushed himself off and jumped back on-board, proclaiming 'Carry on, I'm okay. Take this stage to Medicine Bow.' In a moment where a lesser man might break character, Bang Bang instead came out with a clever reference to the American Western TV series *The Virginian*.

Later in his life, Bang Bang took to introducing himself as 'Lord Dudley, the Divil', managing to both elevate and deprecate himself in a single breath. His eyesight deteriorated with age, and he ended up living in Drumcondra's Clonturk House, a home for the blind run by the Rosminians. In 1979, devastated by the death of his distant soulmate John Wayne, Dudley declared 'me pal is dead.' Eighteen months later, to the day, Ireland's most loveable sniper followed his hero to the great gunfight in the sky.

The whole city was mine.
Everybody knew me and I knew all their faces.
But they had no firearms. I was the only one with a licence.

Bang Bang

Billy in the Bowl

Billy Davis was born without legs, but what he lacked in limbs he made up for with the rest of his body: a big mane of curly black hair, a well-formed mouth, an aquiline nose, Olympic-strength arms and deep, dark eyes like the pools of Heshbon by the gate of Bath-Rabbim. To overcome his handicap, he devised a unique way of propelling himself around Dublin, placing himself in a fortified iron bowl and using two wooden plugs to row himself around the streets as if they were famous Venetian waterways and he a champion gondolier.

He spent some time in the House of Industry, a home for the destitute on James's Street, but was evicted on 1 March 1774 when it was 'deemed and resolved that the man in the bowl dish is not a proper person and is to be discharged from the House of Industry.' So Billy reverted to begging, but eschewed the common targets of the upper class, the gentry and the visitors to Dublin. Instead, he cleverly opted to schmooze with the middle-class servant girls from the country who worked in the big houses of Oxmanstown. His good looks got him in their good books, and they'd happily sneak out leftovers for him. With nowhere else for him to store these scraps, his vehicle/home came to resemble an oversized casserole dish with Billy sitting in the middle of the stew.

Unfortunately, he had a hankering for gambling and drinking, so loose change and spare bits of meat would never be enough to fund this rock star lifestyle. One cold and dark March evening at dusk, he decided to put a novel moneymaking scheme into action. He lay in a hedge along a quiet street, waiting, with his vehicle hidden from view. When a lady – walking alone – came close to his hiding place, he started screaming and crying. Naturally, the good-natured citizen ran to investigate the mystery, when suddenly two big arms emerged from the bush like tentacles from the deep, dragging her in. She promptly passed out from the shock, which gave Billy time to grab her purse, jump into his bowl and flee the scene. When the lady finally came to, she was in such a daze that she was unable to give a description of her attacker. And anyway, nobody would ever suspect a beloved charmer like Billy of such a dastardly deed.

This method of obtaining cash worked a treat until one night outside No. 11 Grangegorman Lane, when he picked on a slightly heftier-than-usual servant girl. She put up a fight, so he had to strangle her to death. When the corpse was found the next morning, it hit all the headlines and Ireland's first ever police force was mobilised – their first mission being to catch 'The Stoneybatter Strangler'.

For a few months, Billy took the sensible option of laying low, but soon his dire financial situation forced him out of retirement. Late at night on Richardson's Lane (now part of the grounds of Collins Barracks Museum, leading towards Arbour Hill), he was passed by two servant girls on their way home from a social evening. Upon spotting the most handsome cripple in all of Ireland, they stopped to admire and take pity on him. 'Aren't you two fine ladies saints to go out of your way to visit a poor prisoner like me?' he remarked, in an eerie moment of prescience.

One of the ladies took out her purse to give him some change, whilst the other installed her glass eye so that she could get a better look at him. The sight of all their fancy things was like a trigger for Billy, so he flung his bowl at one of them whilst throwing himself at the other. But it was still two against one, so one of the ladies managed to grab Billy by the hair, pull a hatpin from her head, and jab it into his eye.

Clothes torn and belongings scattered, they fled the scene to find help. After bumping into a gang of lads on Manor Street and telling them their story, they formed a mob. Together they pushed a wheelbarrow back to where Billy was lying in agony, and triumphantly paraded The Stoneybatter Strangler all the way to Green Street prison.

Thanks to his superhuman strength, Billy managed to avoid the death penalty and was instead employed as a manual labourer for the rest of his life. In his downtime, he was basically a freakshow attraction, as people went along to the jail and had a good gawk at him in his cell.

Billy in the Bowl

Billy Storey

As a child, Billy Storey got his calcium fix sucking the milk straight from the cow's udder. As an adult, he became an outspoken advocate on behalf of pigs, believing them to be just like us human beings (and even better in some respects).

It wasn't only pigs that Billy could philosophise about. In a two-minute conversation, he'd be able to deviate from his thoughts about pig markets and put you right on a variety of other things, which might include politics, drinking, women's rights, the breakdown of the Irish family, the weather and modern milk. 'The milk you buy today is only water,' he'd profess to anyone who'd listen.

Affectionately dubbed 'The Lord Mayor of Manor Street', twice a day he'd command his pony-drawn float through bustling Stoneybatter, loaded with its precious cargo: enormous black barrels of putrid pigswill. He waved to everybody as he went along, basking in the attention that he was guaranteed to attract from curious, nasally-assaulted locals and delighted tourists alike.

It wasn't even unusual for foreigners to abandon their cars in the middle of the street to quickly capture a picture of Billy, seeing this as a unique opportunity that needed to be seized for the benefit of their friends back home. After all, it would be photographic evidence that Ireland – and even its grand capital city – lived up to its twee reputation and was still exactly how their expat great-grandparents had described it.

Billy Storey

The Bird Flanagan

Walter Starkie called him 'Dublin's celebrated playboy', and he once managed to borrow a fiver off King Edward during an important racing event at The Curragh. But who the hell *was* The Bird Flanagan?

Born Willie Flanagan in 1867, this fellow earned his moniker on the day that he went along to a fancy-dress ball in the Earlsfort Terrace roller-skating rink. Some say that he was decked out as a bird, but others claim that he was actually dressed as the Holy Spirit. Either way, when he failed to win a prize for his costume, he climbed up onstage to where the judges sat. Using a rugby ball as a prop, he acted out the animations involved in the laying of an egg, which he then flung at the panel. Ever since that fateful evening, he was exclusively referred to as 'The Bird' and became renowned for his daft antics around town.

In 1907, The Irish International Exhibition was held in Ballsbridge, where Herbert Park is currently. One of the most popular attractions at this world's fair was a human zoo – a Somali village complete with native families, stilt huts, pottery workshops and a schoolhouse. Flanagan visited this exhibit alone, but left with a baby under his jacket. The various legends leave us in the dark about how this charade ended, but we do know that The Bird either a) went drinking with the baby in a Ballsbridge snug, b) wrapped it in a mackintosh and left it in a tramcar at Nelson's Pillar, or c) took it to the French pavilion as a protest against the decline in the French birth rate. Your guess is as good as mine.

The very same year, he rode his horse into the lobby of the Gresham Hotel on O'Connell Street in the middle

24

of the night. Upon requesting a drink from the bar, he was told 'It's after hours, sir,' to which he responded by commanding the horse to jump up on top of the bar, from where he yelled: 'But it's not for me, you fool! It's for the horse!' Despite this audacious act, the hotel bar is now one of two pubs in Dublin named after Flanagan – the other one being in Rialto village.

Outside the pub in Rialto, a sign depicts another one of Willie's famous pranks. One afternoon, he bought a ham that was hanging outside a butcher's shop on Thomas Street. He went into the shop and paid for it, but then left it on its hook and stood beside it for a while. As soon as he saw a policeman coming his way, he grabbed his ham and legged it down the street as fast as his feet could take him. Upon noticing this suspicious behaviour, the policeman had no choice but to take chase, hot on Flanagan's heels. After a long game of cat and mouse, the apparent thief was finally seized, only to express outrage and demand to be brought back to the butcher's shop to prove his innocence. Of course the butcher corroborated Flanagan's story, and the embarrassed and exhausted policeman admitted defeat and released his prisoner.

Always one to hog the limelight, The Bird once rode his long-suffering horse across the stage of a theatre, interrupting a play in the process. Another time, during World War I, he stood up from his seat in the middle of a performance and threw off his overcoat, revealing himself to be dressed as the Kaiser.

Even kids learned to steer well clear of The Bird. Back in those days, owning a football was a luxury known to few children. So when Flanagan presented a young lad with one, along with specific instructions not to tell anybody about the gift, the boy was more than willing to oblige. However, this put the little sportsman into a bit of a tricky situation when he left his new ball at home and showed up at the green, only to be rounded in on by a gang of his disgruntled pals saying 'Where's the ball? The Bird says he gave you a ball for us.'

In another show of selfless generosity, Flanagan gave a shilling to a 5-year-old boy on one condition: that he must immediately go to his mother and tell her 'I just saw a fucking policeman on a horse!' Of course, the stunned mammy gave the boy a box on the ear for spouting such awful language, and fined him a shilling as punishment. It goes without saying that Flanagan's gifts came with more than a few strings attached.

In 1925, The Bird died of pneumonia in Walkinstown House, having lived a leisurely life at the expense of both his wealthy family (who owned cabbage fields all over Walkinstown, Crumlin and Drimnagh) and the good people of Dublin. In his *Irish Times* obituary, he was respectfully referred to as 'an expert agriculturalist, a follower of hounds, and a keen huntsman,' with absolutely no mention of his other side. Perhaps this was an early example of what might be known today as a media cover-up.

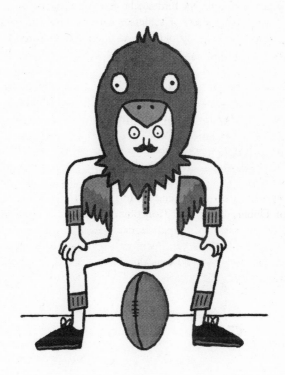

The Bird Flanagan

Boo Paw

For years, this man patrolled the streets of Dublin's north inner city, yelling 'BOO PAW!' at the top of his voice. To the untrained ear, he had the air of a common or garden madman, but the locals were able to make sense of his unfortunate speech impediment and his barking sales pitch. Code cracked, they were able to translate streams of apparent gibberish like 'wan anna boo paw, boo lay, too bus, too pay?' from his native tongue of 'Boo Paw' into English: 'Do you want any boot polish, bootlaces, toothbrushes, toothpaste?'

Many days were known to have been saved when a northside household in crisis mode heard their saviour calling somewhere in the distance the words 'BOO PAW, BOO PAW.' If a suit or a dress needed mending before an important interview, meeting or date, he'd show up – as if by magic – with his gargantuan Mary Poppins-style suitcase, containing within some 'eagle n red' (needle and thread).

If there is a house, there is a door.
Behind that door are people.
People need things… and I have all they need, from a
needle to an anchor.

Bridie

Bridie was both a widow and a cunning entrepreneur who lived on the top floor of a house on Chamber Street. Rumour had it that her only son was serving a long sentence inside a correctional facility, but this isn't what she told people. Like any good Irish mammy would, she claimed that he was away, working in England.

From her modest home, she made a fortune selling all kinds of everything: clothes, shoes, potatoes, fuel, holy statues, and whatever you're having yourself. If you needed a loan of money, she presented a friendlier, more understanding alternative to the professional moneylenders of the time, who could be quite tight and scrupulous.

Despite the stuffed moneybag that she always had tied around her waist, she never upgraded her smelly two-roomed apartment, where she slept in a rocking chair beside the fire. Some say that she was afraid to move house in case her beloved son ever returned and was unable to find his mammy.

Well indeed, one day, he finally arrived home from his 'job' in 'England'. His delighted mother put the rest of her possessions up for sale and, with more than enough money saved for a new life together, they went off to the UK and lived happily ever after…

Or maybe not. A couple of years later, word got back to The Liberties that Bridie had only been gone a week or so when she fell down the stairs and died. It's still unknown what happened to her poor son, and if he ever managed to get over the very sudden and completely unexpected loss of his wealthy old mother.

The Bugler Dunne

In 1899, during the Second Boer War, a 14-year-old soldier by the name of John Francis Dunne became a national hero and the pride of the First Royal Dublin Fusiliers. Whilst fighting in the Battle of Colenso, the Boers attempted to demoralise the British troops by sounding the bugle call that signified for them to retreat. Dunne, smelling a rat, used his initiative and loudly sounded the advance charge instead, receiving a bullet in the arm for his troubles. In the ensuing fracas, the bugle fell from his injured arm and into the Tugela River. Queen Victoria later visited him in hospital to present him with an engraved silver replacement.

Years later, the fully grown Bugler Dunne was arrested in London for obstructing traffic whilst performing his sword-swallowing act. But when his identity was realised by the officials, he was instantly pardoned. Not only that, but he was sent off with £5 from the poor box, as the courtroom thought it was a shame that such a great man had fallen on such hard times. Dunne was also reported to have had some run-ins with the law in Canada. The most curious thing about these episodes is that The Bugler Dunne actually moved Down Under, and lived in Fiji and Australia after the war. The sword-swallower and the Canadian chancer were just two people who cleverly used a well-respected name to help them out of a tight spot.

Back in Dublin, and long after the end of the Boer War (and several other wars in between), another fellow was calling himself The Bugler Dunne – a one-armed, ruddy-faced fellow with long, greasy hair tucked into his collar. However, this man claimed to be the *son* of the boy soldier. He wore a red military coat with a mass of medals pinned to it, allegedly belonging to his father. Perhaps this man was a shy and reluctant war hero himself, as his missing arm was said to have been lost during World War II. He didn't seem to have lost any strength along with the arm, and he was once seen being restrained by six guards (that's twelve arms against one!) outside The Rose Bowl pub, at the corner of Summerhill and Gardiner Street. But despite his own checkered career, he only ever told stories of his father's gallantry, and often received donations on behalf of the famous bugler.

In the post-war era, Dunne was an alcoholic who declined Dublin Corporation's offer to move him a little bit out of the city, to the tenements of Keogh Square in Inchicore. Instead, he assembled a shelter out of lino and wood, and set up house on a patch of wasteland beside Rutland Street National School. The locals referred to this as 'The Dog Box', and would often go dancing in there with Dunne and his girlfriend. It's unknown whether or not he entertained his visitors with the carved bugle that the Queen gave to his dad, but — according to all reports — they were the must-attend social events of the time, with or without any hoity-toity royal artefacts.

Butty Sugrue

On 19 July 1972, Muhammad Ali defeated ex-con Al 'Blue' Lewis after eleven tense rounds in Dublin's Croke Park. Admittedly, the fight was just a distraction for the Irish, who were more excited by the thought that – for a week – they'd be breathing in the same air as the world's most charismatic sportsman. 'Cassius Clay Fever' spread across Ireland that summer, and it was made no less contagious by the revelation that his mother's grandfather was an Ennis man.

The fellow responsible for arranging this 'Second Coming' of sorts was a Kerryman by the name of Michael Sugrue. Aside from his work as a boxing promoter, Sugrue was also a circus performer, wrestler, publican, entrepreneur and strongman. To make up for the fact that he only stretched to around 5'6 in height, he measured around the same in depth and width as well, and it was thanks to his extraordinarily large backside that he became known as 'Butty'.

As a child, he ran away from home to live in a tree, surviving on raw meat, eggs and goat's milk. As long as he lived, this diet never changed. He only lasted a week in his first job, after nonchalantly responding to a simple query from a customer with: 'Sorry, Missus. We've no toilet paper, but we've sandpaper, wallpaper and confetti. Would any of those do?'

After joining Duffy's Circus and spending most of the 1940s touring the country performing prodigious acts of strength, Sugrue earned the title of 'Ireland's Strongest Man'. And when he took up a career as a teetotal publican in London, he became widely acknowledged as *Europe's* strongest man, as he could be regularly seen towing a double-decker bus with his teeth, or lifting a fifteen-stone man with one hand.

In 1966, Nelson's Pillar on O'Connell Street was blown up by republicans. Soon afterwards, Sugrue was spreading the word that Nelson's severed plaster head would be making an appearance in his pub. Excited London-Irish punters swarmed to The Elephant's Head, only to be told that some scoundrels had just stolen the head from a wheelbarrow in the garden.

Whilst running The Admiral Nelson pub in Kilburn, Sugrue devised a new diet and wanted to put it to the test, so he buried his barman Michael Meaney in the yard, with two hoses inserted into his coffin for sustenance. One pipe gave him 1,000 calories of liquid food per day, whilst the other pumped down a fresh supply of Guinness stout. Sixty-one days later, a surprisingly healthy Meaney emerged to the shrill sound of the London-Irish Girl Pipers.

Bringing 'The Greatest' to Dublin was Sugrue's crowning glory, albeit a financial disaster. Despite the hysteria around Ali's visit, only 18,725 people showed up to the stadium, and the shambolic organisation meant that boxing gloves had to be flown in from London at the last minute, as nobody had been put in charge of acquiring them. The fight was staged in aid of charity, and the chosen beneficiary for proceeds was loosely given as 'the mentally handicapped children of Ireland.' Butty, however, lost around £20,000 on the night, so they got nothing.

In 1977, our strongest ever man died as he lived – carrying a fridge upstairs in his pub in Shepherd's Bush.

Cantering Jack

Cantering Jack was a young man who lived in a bush in Dublin in the nineteenth century, and whose sole belongings consisted of a tatty scarlet jacket, multicoloured breeches, a black hunting cap, a fiddle, and a pair of wellies with a rusty spur attached to the back of one.

His cognomen came partially from his equestrian style of dress, and partially from his habit of jumping out of his hedge whenever he spied an approaching carriage of aristocrats. He'd meet them with a wild dance and a jaunty number on the fiddle, and he'd continue the tune as he took chase alongside them. He'd be able to keep up the pace for miles alongside any horse, and would be the travelling party's steadfast entourage until they finally decided to tip him for his musical and athletic prowess. At this point, he would return to his bush.

Captain Dempsey

There once stood a dilapidated wooden hut on a patch of wasteland just off the top of Townsend Street. This was the home of a tall, old man with a beard suggestive of a lifetime's allergy to razors, and sunken, nostalgic eyes that suggested a life long since past its peak.

Born in Cork in 1742, Robert Dempsey was once a powerful adventuring seafarer. But in his bankrupt retirement, the closest he got to castaways, hungry sea-monsters or lost sunken cities was gazing out over the Liffey, and beyond, to the Irish Sea, from the roof of his hut.

Being landlocked in his later years had no bearing on Dempsey's sense of fashion, which was evident from the big silver buckles on his shoes, a plaid shawl around his neck, leather-patched breeches, a broad-rimmed hat and herrings hanging from his cloak. The shallow waters of Dublin Bay used to be a popular bathing spot for schools of herring, but they're a rarer sight nowadays. It's quite possible that the depletion in stock is due to the appetite that Captain Dempsey built up during his wild seafaring days.

Strangely, his rooftop vantage point was also the entrance to his home, which could only be reached by climbing haphazard wooden blocks nailed along the outer wall. Dempsey's unusual brand of architecture was further pronounced by his DIY underground altar, which was kept lit permanently by two oil lamps. It's to here that he'd retreat during his famous meltdowns, for which he became known as 'The Hermit of Dublin'. However, this introversion was sporadic, as he was also famous for engrossing the neighbours in tales about his soap drama love life, his youth spent trading around the West Indies, his 1776 shipwreck off the coast of Newfoundland, and the fleet of ships he had inherited after his uncle's death in Jamaica. He'd be there yapping away when – apropos of nothing – he'd storm underground to his altar (via the roof), slamming the front door on the way.

The locals would spend the next week or so keeping watch for signs of life, and they'd bring him food and drink once he showed his head. It was extremely important to demonstrate even further sensitivity during this charitable act, as he'd fly back into a rage if one were to so much as make eye contact with the rings on his fingers.

There was definitely something about his jewellery, though. Sometimes he'd be leisurely walking down the street, only to stop urgently, stare intently at his rings, mutter something, drop to his knees (rain or shine), take them off and pray to them one by one. Then he'd stand up, brush himself off, and continue along his way through the gawking mob, as if he had done nothing more unusual than stop for a moment to tie his shoelaces.

In 1802 he had one of his usual tantrums, descended into his hideout, took a fit and died. As usual, his neighbours noted his absence, but they were also privy to his ways. And so a week passed before one brave and good samaritan decided to intrude upon the altar of Captain Dempsey, and subsequently discovered his tragic fate.

Corrigan

Every morning from the 1720s to the 1770s, a mule/pony/dog/boy (depending on the decade/day) would drag a cart along to the Church Street bridge. Sitting in the back would be Patrick Corrigan – a very divisive figure amongst Dubliners at the time, known to some as 'His Lowship Prince Hackball', and to others as 'The King of the Beggars.'

Although not born into any royal bloodline, 'The King' was somebody who other beggars looked up to and trusted, and who they would go to for assistance when they needed a dispute adjudicated. He also represented – and spoke on behalf of – his people when they needed to communicate with official authorities. As testament to his social stature, a leading Dublin physician was amongst the witnesses when he married a lady by the name of Alice Lynch in Mary's Lane Chapel in 1731.

In 1744, the parish beadle of Saint Werburgh's Church had him seized, to be brought to the House of Industry. En route, he was rescued by a riotous mob of supporters. And thus began an ongoing tug-of-war between the parish and the 'Friends of Hackball' – a battle that the bad guys eventually won, years later, when they managed to arrest and confine a weakened, elderly Corrigan for good.

Corny Neill

Smithfield resident Corny Neill was a huge fellow who made his living taxiing a jaunting car around Dublin. In the 1930s he was crowned 'King of the Jarveys' (an extremely prestigious title), and became the pride of Queen Street.

The Irish jaunting car had earlier been immortalised in song by Valentine Vousden in the 1850s. Jarveys like Corny could often be heard reciting a verse or two from it (appropriately titled 'The Irish Jaunting Car') in a bid to attract custom.

> *If you want to drive 'round Dublin, sure you'll find me on the stand;*
> *I'll take you to Raheny, for cockles on the strand –*
> *To the Phoenix Park, to Nancy Hands, the monument and then*
> *I'll take you to the Strawberry Beds, and back to town again.*

Crazy Crow

There was a time when Dublin medical schools were constantly in need of fresh corpses to poke and prod, which made the art of bodysnatching quite a lucrative business. This was all thanks to the chapter of the law they called the 'Murder Act', which stated that only the bodies of executed murderers could be dissected.

In 1825, one George Hendrick served time for stealing cadavers from St Andrew's Cemetery. He was a wild-looking, boozy sort, well known for his graveyard manner, and better known as 'Crazy Crow'. When the Anatomy Act of 1832 ruled that students and doctors could now anatomise donated and unclaimed bodies, the bodysnatching industry was made redundant and Crazy Crow was forced to shift industries completely. He became a porter to musical groups and a maker of musical instruments. Working for a theatre, he was required to carry messages, light fires and to make himself generally available to the manager, prompter and performers.

This is how Hendrick came to be more regularly spotted about town carting around a load of trumpets and violins instead of the faithful departed under a mucky blanket. Less understandable, however, is the reason as to why he would hand out photographs of himself to passers-by, accompanied by a rather self-deprecating verse:

> *With a look ferocious, and with beer replete,*
> *See Crazy Crow beneath his minstrel weight,*
> *His voice as frightful as great Etna's roar,*
> *(Which spreads its horrors to the distant shore.)*
> *Equally hideous with his well-known face,*
> *Murders each ear – til whiskey makes it cease.*

Daddy Egan

Daddy Egan was a grey-haired old man who ran a pub on the north side of Smithfield square. He used to stop passing children at random to present them with a prayer sheet and a penny so that they could light a candle in the church on their way home.

Alas, Daddy Egan's pennies were generally sacrificed in the nearest sweet shop rather than for any religious causes, and he unintentionally contributed more towards the rotting of teeth than to the lighting of any candles.

Damn the Weather

Ireland has a temperate oceanic climate that is strongly influenced by the Atlantic Ocean, meaning that we don't experience the extreme temperatures that many other countries on a similar latitude do. Still, despite the relative mildness of the country, you can never please everybody…

There was a time when window-shoppers in The Liberties needed to have their wits about them at all times, as Damn the Weather was liable to appear behind them at any moment. They'd be too engrossed in whatever they were doing to notice the epically bearded man standing next to them preparing for action, stretching his arms out as far as they'd go to achieve maximum span. Suddenly he'd produce a horrifying cacophony of noise like a twenty-one-gun salute, as he stamped his feet on the ground, ferociously slapped both of his hands across his chest, and bellowed 'DAMN THE WEATHER!' into the innocent window-shopper's ear, before fleeing the scene.

This outburst could occur during any weather conditions, at any time of the year. His constant discomfort might have had a lot to do with the fact that he wore a big black overcoat regardless of the season. This might also explain why he seemed to damn the weather slightly more in the summer than he did in the winter.

Dan Donnelly

Dan Donnelly was born on Townsend Street in 1788, the ninth of seventeen children in an understandably poor family. He grew up to be a tall, muscular man, and earned a reputation as a sort of vigilante who put his courage and strength to good use. For example, on one occasion he came to the aid of a young woman who was being attacked by two beefy sailors near the docks – an escapade that he was lucky to come away from in one piece. On another occasion, an elderly lady had died of a highly contagious fever, and people were reluctant to go anywhere near her body for fear of catching it. But Donnelly slung her corpse over his shoulders and gave her a piggyback to the graveyard, where he found two gravediggers at work. They told him that they were working on a plot for a person of distinction, but Dan wouldn't hear of such talk, and he laid the old woman to rest.

One headstrong local boxer who was recognised as 'The Champion of the City' saw Donnelly (and his reputation) as competition, and became adamant that they should fight. After a lot of persuasion Donnelly begrudgingly relented, and, the bout was arranged to be held on the banks of the Grand Canal. Right up until the beginning of the fight, Dan tried to talk his new foe out of competing, but to no avail. Nonetheless, he beat him to the ground in the sixteenth round and was crowned the new 'Champion of the City' in front of a huge crowd of jubilant Dubs.

Having attracted the patronage of aristocrat Captain William Kelly, Donnelly was encouraged to continue with his sporting career, and in September 1814, 20,000 people flocked to see him score a victory over prominent English fighter Tom 'Isle of Wight' Hall. The venue was a natural amphitheatre in The Curragh called Belcher's Hollow, but with Irish pride restored during a time of extremely stressed Anglo–Irish relations, the field was renamed 'Donnelly's Hollow'.

The following year, Donnelly was back in Kildare to fight against another English champion by the name of George Cooper. Five rounds in and Sir Dan seemed beaten, but Captain Kelly's sister – who had bet her entire estate on his victory – slipped a lump of sugar cane into his mouth. That sugar must have had some magical properties, because just a few minutes later Cooper was lying on the ground with a broken jaw.

The victory parade back to Dublin took seventeen days, which works out at around three kilometres per day. This snail's pace wasn't the fault of the four beautiful white horses who pulled the carriage, or the crowds of thousands who thronged the streets. It was because they stopped at every single pub they passed for a celebratory tipple. Donnelly's proud mother sat beside him in the car, and when they finally reached James's Street, she whipped off her top and slapped her breasts, proclaiming 'I'm the woman who reared him, and these are the breasts that fed him!'

With his £60 prize money from the fight, Donnelly became a publican, first setting up shop on Capel Street. Unfortunately, all of his business ventures failed, which might have had something to do with his newfound reputation as a womanising, gambling alcoholic.

He died in 1820 at the age of 31, and his body was laid to rest in Bully's Acre... but only for a few days, as his fascinating corpse was soon exhumed by gravediggers. There was public outrage when the people's champion was found to be missing, and it didn't take long before they found the body in the possession of a surgeon named Hall. Hall agreed to return Donnelly to his grave, on the condition that he could keep his winning right arm for medical observation, which was the beginning of a new lease of life for one of Ireland's most legendary limbs. Over the past 200 years, Donnelly's arm has become a globetrotting curio, having spent time in an Edinburgh medical school, a Victorian circus, a Boston library, New York museums, a Northern Irish folk park, Dublin's Croke Park, and pubs all over Ireland.

Dancing Mary

Mary Margaret Dunne was born in Kilkenny in 1928, was raised in Carlow, and then spent the majority of her life in The Big Smoke. Although she worked as a schoolteacher and a hairdresser, she is best remembered for her dancing. Every single day from the late 1970s until 2002, she could be seen throwing shapes beside the Anna Livia water feature (better known as 'The Floozie in the Jacuzzi') on O'Connell Street. Towards the end of Dunne's tenure, this monument was relocated to the Croppy Acre (near Heuston Station) to make way for the Spire. If this topic were to be broached with Mary, she'd air her stern disapproval of the Spire whilst doling out handfuls of Ritchie's 'Milky Moo' sweets from her handbag.

Mary boogied every day away, ensuring that her footwork always followed the shape of a cross (in honour of the Holy Trinity and the Virgin Mary). There was a time when she'd accompany herself with a sung musical adaptation of the rosary, but she then lost her voice and had to resort to miming instead. Even if Mary wasn't addicted to dancing, she still would've turned as many heads for her quirkily chic dress sense – an unlikely combo of bangles, clip-on earrings, rosary beads, odd gloves, printed scarves, clashing colour palettes, and curly platinum hair laden with scrunchies.

Like any hero, Mary had a nemesis. This came in the form of another holy lady named Annie, who frequented the same area, dressed all in black (complete with beret) and lugged around a large wooden crucifix that she had cloaked in an Irish flag. This woman, however, didn't prove to be as popular with the people of Dublin – quite possibly because she'd randomly chase people down the street and hit them with her cross, with a particular penchant for breaking up young lovers who were holding hands, and chasing down nuns. Mary was also known sometimes to take a stand against religious figures, but she channelled her frustrations in a less physical way, preferring instead to stand up during Mass and heckle the priest if she disagreed with him.

Each and every day, her son drove her from their home in Deansgrange to her dancefloor on O'Connell Street, and then collected her at the end of her shift. She was eventually forced into retirement by her failing eyesight, after over twenty years looking fabulous on the beat, but later remarked that she would 'still dance when I go around visiting friends.'

Mary passed away on St Brigid's Day 2014. Throughout her life she had been affectionately referred to by Dubliners as 'Mad Mary'. After her passing, the slightly more proper and descriptive 'Dancing Mary' became more commonly used by the thousands of people who had been awestruck by her presence.

Dancing Mary

The Dead Man

A patient of St Brendan's psychiatric hospital, The Dead Man would often slip out for a pint in the local pub – O'Dowd's of Grangegorman. Fully convinced that he was no longer of this world, he would tell every patron of the bar that he was dead.

In the same breath that he revealed his bereavement, he'd make sure to suggest that they should buy him a drink and also raise a glass themselves, as an act of veneration. Some customers would doubt his story and think he was a chancer, but would buy him a pint anyway out of respect for the gall of him. But The Dead Man really looked the part – with his blue lips, skeletal face, pale complexion, mouthful of bad teeth, and an extraordinarily peculiar smell emanating from his person. Therefore, others would think it was an awful sin to deprive a dead man of some nourishment, and even worse not to make a toast and to wish him all the best in the afterlife.

With all the free jars he managed to blag, O'Dowd's was like Heaven for The Dead Man.

Decco the Caveman

The unification of Italy in the nineteenth century shattered the feudal land system, which meant that all of a family's territory was to be divided and subdivided amongst heirs. With smaller plots now the norm, it became more difficult to make a living, and there was a sudden spike in emigration. One of the many Italians to land in Ireland during this period was a fellow by the name of Decco.

Decco's best friend was a brown bear who he walked around on a chain and who performed circus tricks for the children of Glenageary, Sallynoggin and Kingstown (now Dun Laoghaire). Whenever the youngsters caught sight of this dastardly duo, they'd leg it home to raid their piggybanks, as they knew that their contribution would help to support and sustain Decco's delightful little enterprise.

One day, Decco's bear passed away. The poor man became a depressed recluse and took to sleeping on a hammock in a disused lead mine on Killiney's White Rock Beach, just down the cliff from where Bono now lives. The next generation of kids who grew up in the area had no knowledge of Decco's showman past, and they'd often tease the poor lad by going down to the beach and yelling 'Decco, Decco!' into his cave – words that would reverberate wildly around his home.

Reports vary as to how he would generally react to these nick-nacks. Some say that he'd emerge from his mine with a vexed and confused expression, whilst other legends suggest that he'd chase these pranksters down the strand wielding an axe. When comparing the ways that two neighbouring generations treated Decco, it's interesting to note how – when it comes to gaining the respect of children – the possession of a cool pet bear can really make all the difference.

Despite the caveman's death towards the end of the nineteenth century, Killiney's abandoned lead mine is and always shall be known to the locals as 'Decco's Cave'. According to some, Ireland's greatest ever hero, Fionn Mac Cumhaill, never died, and is actually resting in a cave beneath Dublin, waiting to re-emerge one day to defend Ireland in our hour of greatest need. Perhaps Decco has joined Fionn in his cave, and now they're both just relaxing and biding their time, until the mighty Fianna sees fit to rise again.

The Diceman

Thom McGinty was born on 1 April 1952, and so he always referred to himself as an 'April Fool'. Originating in Glasgow, he moved to Dublin in 1976 to nude model for life drawing classes in the National College of Art and Design on Thomas Street. With the start date of his job delayed and finances running low, he dressed up as a clown and started sitting in the Dandelion Market (a former bottling plant and stables on Stephen's Green that was converted into a market for hippies and punks). At first, throwing some coins into his bowl would get you a wink, but as McGinty got more confident he started offering better value for money, and would actually perform for his donors. This earned him his first nickname, 'The Dandelion Clown'.

This moniker was quickly forgotten when 'The Diceman' was born, after McGinty took a job that required him to paint his face like a mime and hold a sign advertising 'The Diceman's Game Shop.' One of his tricks was to stand as still as a statue and try to get from the top of Grafton Street to the bottom without anybody noticing him moving – a feat that would usually involve around two hours of miniscule movements. Later in his career, when he started attracting crowds and was constantly getting moved on by the Gardaí, he'd use this statue method to make his getaway, technically obeying the orders which he'd been given, but attracting even more of an audience in the process.

With The Diceman now a beloved street character, he became a much sought-after human statue and was hired to advertise many different products and events. He treated every day like it was Hallowe'en, and you never knew who he was going to be next after you'd seen him around Dublin dressed as a sailor, a condom, a burlesque dancer, Dracula, an ESB lightbulb, the *Mona Lisa*, a clown in a bloodstained robe, a Bewley's teapot, a wizard, Tim Burton's Beetlejuice, a politician, an Easter egg, the Dalai Lama, a tennis ball, an Edwardian news vendor, a house, an An Post postcard, and Norman Bates's dead mother.

Some of his personas had a political tinge, and he became known for his outspoken advocacy of the 'Free Tibet' movement, the freedom of The Birmingham Six, and gay rights (at a time when homosexuality was illegal in Ireland). He wasn't without his detractors though, and in 1991 he was accused of a most terrible offence and charged with a breach of the peace. His crime? One of his costumes consisted of head-to-toe gold bodypaint and a skimpy loincloth that failed to cover his buttocks. Back in those days, this was seen as indecent exposure. In a wonderful twist, the guards who arrested him ended up scrubbing the back seat of their squad-car for hours after dropping him off at the station to remove the golden imprint of The Diceman's arse.

On 20 February 1995, McGinty died tragically of HIV, an illness he'd been diagnosed with in 1990. In his memory, shopping was suspended for an afternoon as his coffin was carried down Grafton Street and hordes gathered to applaud him for one last time. These days, there's a plaque dedicated to The Diceman in Dublin's Meeting House Square, as well as ones in Wicklow and Kerry – testament to how many smiles he elicited all over Ireland. Perhaps the council should go one further and erect a statue of him on Grafton Street – if they did, it might make it into the history books for being the world's very first statue of a statue.

The Diceman

Dingers

Dingers was the minder of a local lady of the night – a woman who was said to have had no shortage of takers. Despite this seemingly lucrative position, Dingers never took a full wallet down to the pub. But this was a minor pitfall, thanks to an ingenious method especially devised to procure free pints: he'd simply walk up to the fullest and freshest drink on the bar, hawk his throat, gather the goods together within his mouth, and propel the vilest of golliers onto the frothed head of the stout.

If the owner of the pint objected to this rather anti-social action, they'd be floored with a punch and then Dingers would relax with his goober-stained, hard-earned beverage. If nobody objected, then nobody would get hurt…

It took a great amount of effort to bring any sort of a halt to Dingers's bad behaviour. Even the police force had a tough time of it. On one occasion backup was called for, but all that meant was that instead of one guard struggling to arrest him, there were soon six guards struggling to arrest him. Fortunately one of the gang was a quick thinker, and he did what anybody in a similar situation would do: he chopped off Dingers's belt. Trousers around his ankles, he was at his most vulnerable and could finally be restrained, much to the joy of the crowd of onlookers who had gathered around the squad car as he was bundled in – many of whom had been forced to donate a few mucous-stained pints to Dingers at some point in their lives.

Doggypond

There's a fenced-off little pond near the cricket grounds of the Phoenix Park, officially known as Citadel Pond. But Dubliners aren't exactly famous for referring to things by their state-given titles. Hence we decided that – because dogs are allowed to be let loose around it – Citadel Pond should be known as 'The Doggy Pond'. Its main claim to fame comes from the fact that the Germans dropped a bomb on it in 1941 (assumedly out of jealousy). Luckily, there were no mutts in taking a dip at the time, but the Nazis *did* manage to destroy the nearby pump attendant's house.

Anyway – there was this fellow in an overcoat who you'd often see near the pond, waiting patiently for a group of tourists to come along and relax on a bench along the bank. As soon as he spotted his prey, he whipped off his jacket like a streaker, leapt into the ice-cold pool and glided towards them, through the murky collected bathwater of Dublin's canine citizens.

Once he got within earshot, he started telling them his inspiring story. Apparently, he was in training to swim the Channel, but first he needed to put together a few quid to help pay for his boat and swimming togs and… well… whatever other stuff people usually need when they're swimming the Channel.

Amazed by the man's athleticism, and more than willing to become patrons of such a heroic sporting achievement, the enthusiastic tourists would happily donate a few dollars (they were usually American) to help him along on his adventure.

In a strange turn of affairs, whenever the park ranger happened to pass by the pond on his rounds, our hero would grab his coat and sprint through the cricket grounds faster than he'd ever swam in his life. Whilst the history books may not list this particular gentleman as having ever crossed the treacherous and lengthy Channel, he certainly managed to clock in a few miles around that doggy-pond. Truth be told, he was probably a more likely contender for an Academy Award than Olympic gold.

Doggypond

Elvis

Far from Graceland are the gaffs of Crumlin, where this fellow would croon Mario Lanza songs as he roamed around the cul-de-sacs. Although he was said to have had slightly Italian features, he was no Gucci model, and was likely to have been living in the Iveagh House (a charitable trust who provided affordable housing for the homeless) at the time.

Not that the suburban housewives of Dublin cared about his appearance, as they rushed to their front doors to hear – as they'd call it – his 'bewwshiful vice'. At the end of each set, they'd send their children out onto the street to pass on a token of their appreciation, overwhelmed and delighted to be getting the Michael Bublé of their generation right on their very own doorstep.

Endymion

James Boyle Tisdell Burke Stewart Fitzsimons Farrell was born in County Louth in 1851. With his lengthy name featuring a nod to almost every clan in Ireland at the time, some referred to him as 'The Irish Mosaic', but he was more commonly known as Endymion. He was said to have come from a Dundalk brewing family, and it seems quite likely that he fell into one of the vats of beer as a child and never fully recovered.

He was always very well dressed, looking resplendent in buckled shoes, a deerstalker hat, a tunic shirt with a red rose in the buttonhole, and white cricket trousers (complete with knee breeches). He also ornamented himself with two leather-sheathed sabre swords, a fishing rod and an umbrella. For whatever reason, his brolly would be unfurled on a nice day and folded away on a wet day, and he was often spotted 'fishing' through the railings of Trinity College as he patrolled his city. He always walked along the kerb, precariously close to the road, making sure that he never strayed inside the lampposts and onto the actual footpath.

Upon reaching the famous Ballast Office clock at the junction of Aston Quay and Westmoreland Street, he saluted to it with one of his swords before setting his own watch to match Ballast time. Then he'd wet his finger in his mouth and hold it up in the air to determine the direction of the wind. Meteorological duties fulfilled, out would come a compass to guide him homeward to Pleasant Street. Even if the compass were to suggest a scenic route via Kilmainham, Chapelizod, Inchicore and Rialto, it's the route that he'd trust and the route that he'd follow.

Even James Joyce took a liking to Endymion, writing several cameos for him into *Ulysses*. At one point in the epic tome, Leopold Bloom and Josie Breen watched as 'a bony form strode along the curbstone from the river staring with a rapt gaze into the sunlight. Tight as a skullpiece a tiny hat gripped his head. From his arm a folded dustcoat, a stick and an umbrella dangled to his stride.' Referring to our hero, Mrs Breen claims that her husband 'will be like that one of these days.' We can only assume that she was eagerly anticipating the day when Denis might possess such a fabulous fashion sense and astute navigational skills.

Endymion

The Female Oddity

The Female Oddity was a lady who only ever wore green, from top to tail. As a child, she ate coal and candles, but her tastes had matured with age to include foods that were far more nutritional and filling. However, her palate remained equally as peculiar, and her adult diet consisted solely of frogs and mice.

Flower

Flower was a poor Jewish man who lived in the Iveagh Hostel and could be spotted rambling around the city most days, always surprisingly well dressed and with a fresh flower in his buttonhole. Despite the fact that he was extremely withdrawn from society, and interacted with nobody, he always had a big bag of currants to share with the kids.

Fluther Good

John 'Fluther' Good was a notorious drinker who lived at No. 58 Foley Street and whiled away his days sitting on a butter-box outside various shops on the Ballybough Road.

One day, Archdeacon Brady – who was involved in the construction of a church in East Wall at the time – called Fluther from his perch to help him lift some sandbags. As a gesture of appreciation for his good deed of the day, the holy man presented him with a magnificent picture of the Sacred Heart of Jesus. The significance of this blessed memento was lost on Fluther, who was in Noctor's of Sheriff Street only hours later attempting to barter the Sacred Heart for a sixpence worth of alcohol. When the barman snubbed his offer, he tried to argue that 'this is what Jesus Christ gave me and you'll take it in payment for my gargle.'

The same pub had a tab for the regulars chalked out on a blackboard behind the bar. One morning, upon opening shop, the barman discovered that they'd been broken into overnight. After an extensive search of the premises, the publican was flummoxed by the apparent burglary, as not a single thing seemed to have been stolen. The mystery lingered until he later spotted the slate of debtors behind the bar, and noticed that Fluther Good no longer owed them a large sum of money. In fact, Good's name had bizarrely disappeared from the list overnight. The barman didn't require Holmesian powers of deduction to work out who the culprit might have been.

In 1926, Seán O'Casey presented to the Abbey Theatre his latest work, *The Plough and the Stars*, which features a character called Fluther Good – a brave, passionate and humorous carpenter and trade unionist who often serves as the voice of reason within the play. Alas, the character's namesake was unimpressed. Years later, John Ford's Hollywood adaptation of the play was released, and actor Barry Fitzgerald received international acclaim for his portrayal of Fluther. This was the last straw for the *real* Fluther, and he began legal proceedings against O'Casey. When a 1937 edition of the *Sunday Chronicle* broke the news about the lawsuit, Fluther decided that he'd also sue the newspaper for libel, taking umbrage at their headline: 'Barry Fitzgerald Tells of Dublin Wag's Threat of Law Action.'

According to Good, being labelled a 'wag' had resulted in him being 'ridiculed and lowered in the estimation of his friends and other members of the public.' Assumedly, these friends and other members of the public were unaware that the same man had once broken into a pub solely to erase his drinking debt from a chalkboard.

The Gatekeeper

The Gatekeeper used to roam around the streets of Rathmines and Ranelagh all day, making sure that the front gate of everybody's garden was closed. As she went about this crucial duty, she'd be constantly nibbling on a slice of stale bread for sustenance, with a seemingly unlimited supply of the stuff in her pocket.

Granny Dolan

The death of a loved one can be an emotionally crippling experience, and often a financially crippling one as well. So it's just as well that Manor Street had a local hero whose name reflected her motherly commitment to the community.

Granny Dolan would look after the recently deceased. She'd down a few Baby Powers (miniature whiskeys) and get to work – washing, shaving and dressing the corpses to make them look a bit more presentable for their journey to the afterlife. As testament to her kindness, Dolan never looked for any compensation for her morbid duties... except for maybe another whiskey or two when the job was done.

Hairy Lemon

Hairy Lemon was a formidable dog-catcher who patrolled the city around the time of World War II, permanently flanked by a freshly gathered collection of canines and named after his easily recognisable ginger head and curious skin tone. But it wasn't just mutts who he went after, as bold children would often be told by their parents to 'behave yourself, or else Hairy Lemon will get ya.' Daring children were known to heckle him on his rounds, retreating to a safe distance and yelling: 'Hairy Lemon, has your mother got any more like you?'

Hairy Lemon's most commonly reported stomping ground was in the vicinity of The Big Tree pub in Drumcondra. Although his nickname could probably be accredited to a stylistic grooming decision on his part, it's now known that alcoholic hepatitis can cause jaundice, which might go some way towards explaining his curious yellow complexion.

Despite being under the employ of the council, Hairy Lemon was of no fixed abode and often relied on handouts from the nuns in Cabra's Dominican Convent. When he passed away in the 1950s, a kind local librarian paid to have a Mass offered in his memory. Unaware of his actual name, and thinking that it might be uncouth to refer to a deceased human being as 'Hairy Lemon' in a place of worship, the priest that day prayed for the salvation of the soul of an enigmatic-sounding individual called 'H. L.'

Hairy Lemon

Hairy Yank

The Wall Street Crash of 1929 had different effects on different people. Due to the events of Black Tuesday, businesses closed down, jobs were lost and America was plunged into the Great Depression. It ruined bankers, brokers and speculators to the extent that some of them felt the need to shoot themselves, drink poison, jump off buildings or smother themselves in gas-filled rooms.

One previously wealthy fellow left broke by the collapse decided that money wasn't worth dying for, and instead he relocated to Dublin and became a cabbage plant salesman. Because of his hairstyle and his heritage, he became known locally as Hairy Yank.

He made it his job to go door-to-door, offering households the chance to have their own personal cabbage patch, which would provide a family with a steady supply of the vegetable for not much more than it would cost to buy a few of them fully grown down at the grocer's. Because he called during the day, the man of the house was generally out at work, and Hairy Yank only had to sell himself to the housewives of Dublin. Once his generous offer was on the table, he'd sweeten the deal even further with his smooth American charm, exotic accent and cunning use of compliments. 'If they saw you over in Hollywood, you'd be their biggest star!' he'd say, to a reception of blushes and giggles.

Transaction complete, he'd go out into the lady's back garden to plant a hundred cabbages. That night, he'd return in the darkness to dig them all up again. The next day, he'd be walking up the very same street fixing his hair, preparing to do it all again with the woman next door.

Questionable though his ethics may have been, the parable of Hairy Yank teaches a great lesson about how you should never give up, because there's always a new opportunity waiting just around the corner – and no matter how dire your financial situation may be, there's always someone gullible waiting to be ripped off.

Hamlet, Dunbar and Uncle

In the 1860s, Dublin had a little fellow by the name of O'Brien who sang topical songs such as 'Donnybrook is No More', a tune about the closure of Donnybrook Fair. O'Brien was also a very convincing Shakespearean actor, and that's how he came to be more commonly known as 'Hamlet'.

On weekends, he was joined by two of his buddies – rag-and-bone men, who made a living scavenging through the city in search of unwanted household items that they could then sell on to manufacturers and merchants. They were 'Uncle' (as he'd often be heard from miles around bellowing T. S. Lonsdale's music hall standard 'Tommy, Make Room for Your Uncle') and 'Dunbar'. Together, Hamlet and Uncle would harmonise on ballads like 'The

Policemen's Whistles', whilst Dunbar kept the beat with a set of bones in each hand.

In 1874, Dublin hit fever pitch in anticipation of a visit from celebrated American evangelists Dwight L. Moody and Ira D. Sankey. In their honour, Hamlet penned 'A New Song on the Happy Return of Moody and Sankey', where he referred to them as 'timble riggers' (a name given to swindlers who operate the infamous 'Three Shells and a Pea' game), 'morphidites' (a bastardisation of the word 'hermaphrodites') and 'horrible scoopers'.

Some time later, on the occasion of the evangelists' departure from Ireland, our trio sang 'The Souper's Lament for the Loss of Moody and Sankey'. Just a few decades previously, during the Great Famine, 'souper' had been the derogatory term used for anybody who had converted from Catholicism to other Christian denominations in exchange for food. It was obvious that the musicians' opinion of the religious pair hadn't changed a whole lot.

Hamlet, Dunbar and Uncle always said whatever they felt like saying through the medium of song, no matter how controversial it may have been. In hindsight, it might seem that they were three of our very first punk rockers.

Harry Lipman the Ragman

The workforce of the rag-and-bone industry traditionally consisted of down-at-heel gentlemen who had been forced into the most menial of work. This generalisation didn't apply to Harry Lipman, who was said to have been 'a millionaire', and who had his own scrapyard off Brunswick Street, from where he sorted and sold bottles, rags, jars, tins, boards, beds and furniture. He even had his own workforce – a team of ladies who were required to cut the lining out of old clothes and wash out jars, all the while singing their personal anthem:

> *Down in Harry Lipman's yard,*
> *Where the girls are working so hard –*
> *We don't give a damn,*
> *We get money for jam,*
> *Down in Harry Lipman's old yard.*

Lipman never took a break for himself. Even on holidays, he'd be working away inside the yard with the gates closed. If he ever had a spare moment, he'd pop across to O'Connell Street to preach about religion from atop a box.

He wasn't a miser either. He sent off dosh to the Middle East to help provide aid to victims of the conflict, and – although not technically a 'moneylender' – he was happy to help people out with a loan if it was required for something noteworthy, like a Confirmation, Communion or funeral. Upon his retirement, he trusted his entire business to his top assistant, Jimmy Byrne, who referred to his old boss as 'the Godfather of all the Jews in Dublin.'

The Haymarket Players

Every Wednesday at 5 p.m., a married couple would wheel their barrel organ through Smithfield and put on a thirty-minute show, starting off on Haymarket before moving to Benburb Street for Act II.

The man would wordlessly turn the handle of the organ, cranking out saccharine ballads and music-hall standards like '(You're My Heart's Desire, I Love You) Nellie Dean', 'Sweet Rosie O'Grady' and 'Peggy O'Neill'. Young ladies and small children would gather round and dance down the road to the joyous tones, whilst the grown-ups would poke their heads out their front windows or stand on their doorsteps to listen. Meanwhile, the organ grinder's wife wandered about holding out a cloth bag, soliciting donations. Good parents would send their children out with a penny for the pair.

All of the songs on these organs were pre-programmed, so there'd be no chance of an improvised jam or an encore from The Haymarket Players, and at half past five on the dot, the man would shut the side of the organ and pull it away, followed by his wife. It was like the circus leaving town, and Smithfield would fall (relatively) quiet until the same time the following week.

Hector Grey

According to Dublin historian Éamonn Mac Thomais, Hector Grey was 'a household name in Dublin, nearly as well known as the Ha'penny Bridge.' Fittingly, it was just north of the bridge – outside the Woollen Mills – that the small bespectacled man began to make his name (although his *real* name was actually Alexander Scott, and he was born in Scotland in 1904).

Standing on a box, he'd sell all sorts of bric-a-brac and novelties, with an elaborate freestyle spiel about each individual item. Something that would allegedly cost ten shillings 'in the shops' would be offered to the gathering crowd for half that – and if there were no takers, the price would begin to slide even further downwards. Sometimes he'd even provide a live demonstration to encourage the opening of wallets. If a small pair of scissors was up for grabs, Grey would show off how well they cut his nails; if it was a mouth organ being auctioned, potential customers would be treated to a few sample melodies.

As his business grew, he set up shop on Upper Liffey Street and became a known 'Wholesaler of Fancy Goods', visiting countries like Japan, Singapore and Taiwan to hunt down bargains and import new products directly. To a child, Hector Grey's was like a treasure trove, and without his reasonably priced merchandise a whole generation of Dubliners may have been deprived of a visit from Santa Claus on Christmas Eve.

For over fifty years (until his death in 1985), Grey gave Dubliners what they wanted, for a fee they could afford. That said, he could've sold crisps to Mr Tayto himself, and he's now fondly remembered with a plaque on the spot where he first traded.

Hoyer Kelly

This old-fashioned gentleman earned his nickname through his cordiality, as he would politely greet everybody who he passed. Of course, any Dub with half an accent has the capability of turning the simple phrase 'how are you?' into something like 'howaya' or 'hoyer'.

According to popular legend, he had fought with the Irish Guards during World War II. After a successful tour of duty, he returned home shell-shocked to find that his girlfriend had only gone and gotten married to some other fellow. Destitute and lonely, Kelly spent the rest of his days wandering around Dublin with his trusted companion, Rusty the Dog, relying on the benevolence of the good samaritans of north inner-city Dublin. Tragically, Hoyer and Rusty were both killed in a fire in the 1960s.

Later that decade, James Plunkett – writing his great novel *Strumpet City* – paid tribute to Hoyer in the form of the wonderfully philosophical and free-spirited tramp Rashers Tierney (expertly portrayed by David Kelly in the subsequent TV adaptation). Rashers even had his own cute little constant sidekick, and Plunkett didn't even bother to change *his* name. Sadly – SPOILER ALERT – Rashers and Rusty met their end in circumstances that were just as heartbreaking as the demise of their real world counterparts.

Jack Plant

Jack Plant and his female friend lived together in a bedsit on Moore Street, from which clattering and screaming always seemed to emanate. He was a Shakespearean actor who permanently spoke like he was up on stage reciting a soliloquy in front of a sold-out theatre.

Rather than packing out The Gate or The Abbey, he'd wander around the city late at night with his big Alsatian dog (for security purposes). Then up to total strangers he'd go, to regale them with stories about his troubled domestic life and all of the terrible insults he'd been given and all the awful names he'd been called by his partner (or 'that denizen of the deep,' as he called her). With great pride, he'd also tell his new friend(s) about his incredibly witty retorts, which had eventually won him the argument.

Whether his audience had any actual interest in hearing the nitty-gritty details of Jack's love life was irrelevant, and every night he'd go out onto the city streets to perform his latest one-man show.

Jack the Tumbler

Dressed in his claw-hammer coat, barefoot and bearded, Jack stood guard on the Conyngham Road, just outside the Phoenix Park. He'd bide his time until a hackney appeared on the road (or better yet, a wedding entourage heading from the church in Dublin to the afters in Lucan). This was his cue for the performance to commence.

He'd fall over and tumble alongside the vehicle for a few moments. Upon noticing this bewildering spectacle, the travelling party would often throw a copper or two in his direction – not out of appreciation, but in the hope that this might help to get rid of him. Sure enough, when Jack heard the clinking of the coins hitting the ground, he'd finish with his act and would start making tracks towards the local snug, royalties in hand.

An elderly lady once complained to the police that she was fed up with Jack carrying out this charade outside of her house. Jack protested that he'd only been doing a couple of tumbles, and that he'd been paid a penny in return for them, so that made it a legitimate purchase of services. The deciding constable ruled that – as per the Vagrancy Act – Jack technically wasn't begging, but that he was simply following his natural calling (which just so happened to be tumbling alongside traffic).

The constable kindly suggested to the lady that she could apply for a court injunction if she wished to keep Jack the Tumbler away from her house, but that he was personally powerless to stop him. Unimpressed, she watched the pair as they walked off, muttering 'Damn him and his injunction. One is as bad as the other.'

Jembo No-Toes

When Jembo returned from World War I, he was blind, shell-shocked and missing several toes. As a result of his eponymous foot problem, he had bad balance and would shuffle down Patrick Street and around The Liberties singing an ode, which must have been stuck in his head for many a year…

> *I don't want to go to the trenches no more,*
> *Where the alley man's guns shatter and roar.*
> *Oh my, oh me, take me home over the sea,*
> *Back to The Liberties.*

Periodically, sometimes even mid-song, he'd lose his cool apropos of nothing and start screaming and shouting – a symptom of the shell-shock. Once, a local comedian by the name of Osso Dougherty thought it would be a lark to steal Bang Bang's key and to promise to return it on the condition that he was daring enough to stick-up Jembo No-Toes.

So, the next time Bang Bang saw Jembo on the street, he snuck up behind him and let out a huge roar into his ear. Memories of bombs and grenades and rifles must have flooded Jembo's consciousness, as he went ballistic and gave chase to Bang Bang (he himself also lacking in vision). This eventually culminated in a standoff inside a concrete bomb shelter on Weavers' Square, where Jembo gave Lord Dudley the whack of a brass bar that had fallen off a discarded bed. Knowing Bang Bang as well as we do, it's fair to assume that he probably thought that this was all just a bit of fun. But poor Jembo had obviously been wrong to assume that The Liberties was any safer than the trenches.

Jenny with the Dogs

Anybody who grew up around Dublin 15 in the late twentieth century would be familiar with Jenny Powell, who'd wander around Blanchardstown with a pack of smartly dressed dogs, pushing a buggy occupied by a goat.

If your family dog was old or poorly – and you were of an age that you were unaccustomed to death and all of its trappings – there's even a likelihood that your parents told you they were sending the dog to live with Jenny, before they secretly brought him/her on its ultimate visit to the vet. The thought of your pet going to live with a gentle old lady like Jenny was far preferable to the idea of it receiving a lethal injection.

Her English accent gave way to unsubstantiated rumours that she was from a wealthy British background, and another whisper that she was a witch meant that none of the locals would ever cross her, for fear of having a spell cast upon them. She actually lived with her zoological family in a caravan on the back-roads between Blanchardstown and Finglas.

As Blanchardstown expanded and became a hub for a number of multinational corporations, the site on which her caravan was parked became sought after by property developers and the council. Despite several generous offers, Jenny refused to budge and continued to beg for a livelihood, but always ensured that her pets were well looked after before spending a penny on herself. Although it's still up for debate whether or not she was an aristocratic sorcerer, she was most definitely a philanthropist, as her animals always looked warmer, perkier and better nourished than their foster mother. Whenever a Meals-on-Wheels volunteer delivered a hot, healthy dinner to her home, the majority of it went straight down on the floor for the happy little goat to devour.

If only Jenny had been around a few decades earlier, she might have met her dream man. In the 1930s, a gentleman named Arthur lived with an army of cats in a handmade shack near the railway tracks in Cabra, off Fassaugh Avenue. Like Jenny, he was an enigma to the locals, spoke with a well-educated English accent, and his sole purpose in life seemed to be providing for his cats. He even walked into town every day to fetch a fresh parcel of meat for his feline friends. What a wonderful pair they would have made!

Joe Edelstein

A hundred years ago, the Jewish population of Ireland was about three times as large as it is now. In fact, the area around Portobello, Clanbrassil Street and the South Circular Road was known as Dublin's Jewish Quarter, or 'Little Jerusalem'. One of the most influential figures in the community at the start of the twentieth century was a businessman and writer by the name of Joe Edelstein.

At the inaugural meeting of the Judeo-Irish Home Rule Association in the Mansion House in 1908, he was vocal about supporting 'such measures as will tend to secure for the people of Ireland a full grant of self-government.' This was just the start of much Jewish-Irish camaraderie in the struggle for Irish independence – a kinship that is often overlooked and forgotten about.

The same year, Edelstein published a book entitled *The Money Lender*, a dark and scurrilous portrait of the fictional Moses Levenstein, with questionable cover art by Phil Blake. This work didn't exactly go down a treat with his contemporaries, as many local Jews thought that it reinforced some of the unflattering racial stereotypes from which they had been trying to distance themselves. To Edelstein's credit, he was trying to make a point about how those who entered into the shady moneylending industry were themselves reinforcing stereotypes, and doing little to aid their community's integration into Irish society.

Despite this controversy, he remained a prominent character around town – even becoming the first Jewish editor of the *Labour Gazette* – until he fell on some hard times. He was fond of 'red biddy' (a concoction of red wine and methylated spirits) and prone to psychiatric breakdowns, which resulted in several long-term stays in the Richmond Lunatic Asylum. He was often on the wrong side of the law, and served some time for indecent assault, being drunk and disorderly, spying, damaging works in the National Library, and discharging firearms in a place of entertainment. However, there was another crime for which he was regularly punished, but it was a charge that he provoked – and even welcomed – every time.

Back in those days, if you needed the assistance of a fire brigade, you went along to a red lamp-post, broke the glass on it to sound the alarm, waited patiently for the services to arrive, and then directed them to the scene. The penalty for sounding a false alarm was either a £5 fine or a night in the cell. Being homeless and broke, Edelstein repeatedly smashed the glass, knowing that if he did the crime, he'd have to serve the time. To him, this just meant a free taxi service and a B&B for the night. He pulled this stunt with such regularity that the fire alarm on Clanbrassil Street became known to the local firefighters as 'Joe's Alarm'.

Ironically, he was hit by a fire truck and killed in 1939. His gravestone, which can be found in the Jewish cemetery in Dolphin's Barn, is inscribed with the words 'many were his good deeds.' When word of his death reached his family – who were living in Canada – his brother, Ernie, thought that their mother might die if she heard the bad news. And so for the rest of her life, Ernie kept his brother alive, forging letters to her – from Canada to Canada, via Ireland – with the sign-off 'Your son, Joe'.

Joe Sadler

Joe Sadler was a blind fellow who lived on Barrack Street (now Benburb Street) who, at some point in his life, made the career change from street poetry to newspaper sales. Being blind and a newspaper salesman might sound like an unlikely combo, but he was able to tell the difference between all of the different papers from the feel of them.

Every day, he'd get a friend to tell him all of the front-page headlines so that he could yell them out to advertise his wares. Unfortunately, some of his friends fancied themselves as part-time comedians, and Sadler would often be heard breaking the most outrageously nonsensical news stories to the people of Arran Quay: 'Shipping Disaster in Dublin Bay – Hundreds Dead', or maybe even something like 'Bigfoot Spotted in the Phoenix Park', 'Bang Bang Arrested in Connection with Shooting' or 'Ireland Win the World Cup.' You'd never know what huge scoop Joe Sadler was going to come out with next.

Once you'd purchased a newspaper from him and you were heading off home, you had to be careful in saying goodbye. A wise person would soon learn the etiquette for doing so. If you said 'Goodnight, Joe,' he'd reply with a friendly 'Goodnight, my son,' but if you said 'Goodnight, Sadler,' he'd mutter and curse after you as you wandered off with your evening news.

Johnny Fortycoats

Every area of Dublin seems to have had its own 'Fortycoats' at some point or another, but P. J. Marlow was the original and the best. Despite his nickname, Marlow only ever actually wore three or four tatty overcoats at any one time, but it certainly gave the illusion of more. As he slept rough, this swaddling was usually necessary for warmth, but – oddly enough – he retained the same number of layers all year round. This meant that there was an awful stink off him, and you'd be cursing if you ended up on the same bus or in the same pub as him.

Some of the kids thought it was a bit of a laugh to get a chase off him, knowing full well that he'd never be able to catch them, what with all of his baggage. So they'd yell at him, 'Hey, Johnny, how many coats are ya wearin' today?' and then take off, roaring with laughter. The younger kids were less brave, as they'd often be threatened by their parents that 'if you don't eat your vegetables, Fortycoats will come and get you' or 'if you don't stop crying, Fortycoats will put you under his coat and you'll never be seen nor heard of again.'

His favourite place to loiter was on the corner of Dirty Lane (now known as Bridgefoot Street), where he'd stand with his cane in one hand and a tin can in the other, soliciting donations. As well as his stick, his can and his coats, Marlow always seemed to be burdened with a load of extraneous tat and clutter. Some say he was a great reader, and others say he had 'a face like Jesus Christ himself' (despite his tight haircut and clean-shaven face). One thing he was well known for was going into a restaurant, ordering what he wanted, throwing down a wad of notes and then making himself at home – assuming of course that putting your feet up on the seat and spitting on the floor was something that you might do in the comfort of your own home. This practice gave him a bad reputation with restaurateurs around town, and meant that he soon ran out of cafés that would accept his custom.

It's unknown if Marlow is the same 'Fortycoats' who used to go door-to-door in Cabra, begging for tea in a slightly unorthodox fashion, but this other chap is also worthy of a mention. He'd ask for a lend of a cup in one house, some tea in the next, a dash of milk from their neighbour, and then finally some sugar, resulting in the perfect cup of tea. It must be said that this story speaks volumes for the generosity of the people of Cabra, considering that he was able to successfully obtain a perfect cuppa from four different houses without the brew going cold.

The legend of Fortycoats became so popular that a fictionalised version of the character even appeared in RTÉ's classic children's TV show *Wanderly Wagon*, as well as a spin-off series entitled *Fortycoats & Co.* In the latter broadcast, Fortycoats was the captain of a flying sweet shop, which he navigated around Ireland, fighting evil. Back in the real world, some eyewitnesses say that Marlow ended up relocating to Harold's Cross in his later years – but then again, this could have easily been one of his many namesakes.

Johnny Fortycoats

Johnny Rea

Johnny Rea aka 'Ray' is fondly remembered as a native of Italy who made his own delicious ice cream in Smithfield, which he sold from a barrel into wafers and cones. He later relocated to the Cornmarket area, where he continued to cater for the sweet-teeth of Dubliners on their rare sunny days.

Ray shouldn't be confused with another cart-based ice cream vendor from around the same time whose specialty flavour was 'raspberry ripple'. This fellow had a cyst on the back of his hand, and some knowledgeable insiders would have you believe that this sore was the source of the ripple. For those who preferred their iced treats to be strictly vegetarian and free of any secret ingredients, Johnny Rea was the man to keep an eye out for when the sun came out to play.

Jonny Farthing

In the days before decimal currency, there used to be twenty shillings in a pound, twelve pennies in a shilling, and four farthings in a penny. So Jonny Farthing used to offer a great deal, because whenever you met him, he'd happily give you a penny in exchange for a farthing.

Lilian McEvoy

Poor Lilian McEvoy was a Kells-born street musician who was constantly being deemed a nuisance and moved along by the Gardaí. Amongst her known patches were O'Connell Street, Earl Street, Marlborough Street and Grafton Street, but she was never permitted to get comfortable with any one of these places for very long. One evening in 1932, the world-renowned classical composer Fritz Kreisler was strolling down Grafton Street when he heard McEvoy singing and stopped in his tracks. Highly impressed by her voice, Kreisler hooked her up with a week's work performing in the Theatre Royal on Hawkins Street.

Meanwhile in Bournemouth (in the south of England), a dance band leader by the name of Charlie Douglas was eating fish and chips out of a newspaper, which happened to contain a heart-warming story about the chance meeting of Kreisler and McEvoy. Intrigued, Douglas set about checking out this prodigious new talent (as soon as he finished his dinner, of course).

The pair ended up getting married, and by the 1950s they were touring Ireland as 'The Douglas–McEvoy Trio', with their young daughter, Shirley, completing the group. Little Shirley Douglas later went on to achieve considerable success as part of the British skiffle revival, a craze that came about when English jazz musicians took inspiration from African-American country blues and went back to using cheap – often home-made – instruments. Lonnie Donegan became the poster boy of the scene, and a young Liverpudlian skiffle group called The Quarrymen went on to some success after changing their name to The Beatles.

Perhaps it's a stretch to suggest that An Garda Síochána are responsible for the existence of The Beatles – but they can take at least some credit for the skiffle revival, as if it weren't for their intolerance of street musicians, one of the stars of the genre would never have been born.

Lino

This fellow used to lie on the ground all over the city, like some sort of human linoleum. So, naturally, he ended up being known as 'Lino'.

Liverpool Annie

Liverpool Annie was a prostitute who worked around the docks in the 1960s, and by all accounts was an exceptionally attractive one too. This was despite the fact that she got her beauty sleep in cars left overnight outside of a garage on the quays, or, failing that, in a shed next to the weighbridge. To keep herself clean, she'd walk down the steps along the quayside wall and bathe in the revitalising waters of the River Liffey. For optimal cleaning coverage, she would perform this activity topless (even in the wintertime), and many young Dubliners' first pubescent awakening came when they happened to be alongside the river during Annie's bath time. If she was on the other side of the city and needed a wash, it was the people who passed by the horse trough on Watling Street who were in for a treat.

Some of the dockers knew her as 'Penny', in reference to the bargainous price she was rumoured to charge. Her more widespread nickname came about on the night that a ship arrived to the port from Liverpool, and Annie was the only pavement hostess on duty. Always one to keep the customer satisfied, she was happy to cater for every member of the crew herself.

Despite her level of destitution, Liverpool Annie came from a Romanian background and was well able to look after herself. Once, when an imprudent fellow called her 'mad', she put a Gypsy curse upon him, claiming that his firstborn child would be born mad, as penance for their father's cruel slur.

Liverpool Annie

Love, Joy and Peace

In the 1930s, Love, Joy and Peace spread his beautiful message around on the pavements of Dublin. Whenever we were lucky enough to experience even the briefest moment of dry weather, this fella could be seen hunched over a large patch of ground with a Dublin flag and an Ireland flag hanging out of his haversack – a bag that he kept jam-packed full of art supplies.

A huge motivational shamrock of chalk was his calling card, with words etched onto it to differentiate from the famous clover of St Patrick; the green leaf on the left espoused 'love', the white leaf in the middle preached 'joy', and the orange leaf on the right longed for 'peace'. Given what we know about the events of this turbulent era, it's sad but likely that Love, Joy and Peace's message failed to reach the people who needed to hear it the most.

Lugs Branigan

Jim 'The Bran' Branigan was a boxer with cauliflower ears, unwillingly nicknamed 'Lugs' due to his affliction. He joined An Garda Síochána in 1931, at the age of 21, and with his unique methods – many of which could only have existed in a world prior to the founding of a Garda Ombudsman – he soon established himself as the city's most famous law enforcer.

If he caught a pair of eejits fighting, he'd break them up and force them to shake hands. If he caught a scalper selling tickets outside the National Stadium at over-inflated prices, he'd offer to 'help' him and would then flog the tickets at face value. Once they were all sold, he'd give the proceeds to the unamused tout and would walk off, acting as though he had just performed his good deed for the day. When it came to slightly more illicit felons who ended up back at the cop shop, he would offer first-time offenders the option of a night in the cell or a box in the face (after he was crowned Leinster Heavyweight Champion in 1937, it's likely that the first choice became the more popular one).

When the printers' strike of 1934 left a lot of young people (especially newsvendors) unemployed, this mass redundancy led to the emergence of 'Animal Gangs' around the city. Armed with home-made weapons like lead-filled tyres and blade-laden potatoes, these gangs plunged Dublin into a period of unrest, and Branigan was the only man for the job. When Lugs arrived at the scene of a riot, it'd be like Moses parting the Red Sea. He'd walk right up to the biggest troublemaker he could spot, and he'd knock him to the ground with a single punch. Everyone there would instantly know not to try anything clever, and the situation would be defused.

Lugs made even more of a name for himself after the 1940 Battle of Baldoyle (a grisly day at the races, spurred on by a rivalry between two bookmakers) and the 1942 Battle of Tolka Park (another premeditated, unsporting affair, this time between the Ash Street gang and the Stafford Street gang). These infamous incidents made national news at the time – demoting World War II to the middle pages of the papers – and Lugs played a central role, restoring order on the day and giving evidence in the courtroom afterwards. He also made international news when he was bitten on the bottom by an arrest-resisting thug, and then jokingly claimed in court that 'he was worse than the Balubas – at least they cook you first.'

In the following decade, dandily dressed Teddy boys appeared on the scene, causing a nuisance on street corners and rioting in cinemas during screenings of *Rock Around the Clock*. This movie – based around the discovery of rock and roll music – was known for putting adolescents in the mood for devilment, and Branigan's job required him to see the film over 125 times. Most of these would have been incomplete viewings, interrupted by fights and the destruction of cinema property, but it's still safe to say that Lugs wouldn't have been Bill Haley's biggest fan. He was also weary of the Showband scene, once remarking that those types of groups 'attract a bad crowd, real bowsies.'

He was the leader of the Riot Squad, mobilised in 1964, who patrolled the city, quelling any disputes they happened upon. One evening, a group of defenceless Trinity students were attacked and karate-kicked by a gang of hooligans with frying pans, belts, metal bars and glass bottles. The arrival of Lugs's team wasn't before four of the students were seriously injured, ending up in hospital. Despite the carnage, Branigan referred to this as 'a quiet night.'

He was obsessed with logging the first charge of every year, so if it was panning out to be a quiet New Year's Eve and he happened to arrest somebody at 10 p.m., he'd drive them around chatting to them until midnight, when he'd finally book them. Surprisingly, even the criminals were happy with this arrangement, one of whom noted that 'being the first lawbreakers of a new year, you were guaranteed good exposure.'

Branigan's good rapport with law-abiding citizens meant that he became a guardian to many. He was accredited with saving a number of marriages in The Liberties by giving errant husbands their 'last warnings'. Looking back on his career, he said 'there was just one thing I couldn't stand for, and that was a man beating a woman.' His refereeing of over 13,000 boxing matches obviously contributed to his skills of mediation, and he was often called upon for help and advice, becoming a sort of King Solomon of The Liberties. Bizarrely, on his last night of duty before retirement in 1973, the prostitutes of Dublin (whom he respectfully referred to as 'pavement hostesses') made a hoax emergency call to lure him to the Pepper Canister Church, where they presented him with a fancy cutlery set and a signed card.

Mad Moses

With a 'Nicorette' branded knitted cap on his head, and a contradictory cigarette between his lips, Mad Moses put plastic bags over the bins of Dublin and then stood guard until somebody required use of the disposal facility. If you wanted to throw something away, you'd have to go through Moses first.

By making himself the middleman in these trash transactions, he gave himself the honour of deciding which items actually deserved to be got rid of and which ones he'd inherit for himself. In doing so, he actively proved the point that Hector Uquhart once prudently made: one man's rubbish truly is another man's treasure.

The Man on the Bridge

In the late nineteenth century, with an increasingly anti-Semitic atmosphere on the continent, the Feldmans – a Ukrainian Jewish family – fled from Kiev to Dublin on a horse-drawn carriage. In 1901, Abraham Feldman was born. Even in Ireland, there was some stigma attached to having a Jewish-sounding name, so the Feldmans – desiring to integrate more effectively into society – became the Fields. Accordingly, the family changed their forenames too. Abraham became Arthur, Jacob became Jack, Moses became Maurice, Hezekiah became Harry, and David... well... even then, David was a common enough name, and he got to keep the name he was born with.

As an enterprising young man, Arthur set up a little studio off O'Connell Street where Dubliners could record the sound of their voices. Unfortunately, most people living here during this volatile period were unable to afford such a luxury. Ever the innovator, Fields got his hands on a box camera in the 1930s and took to the streets, and to the only bridge in Europe as wide as it is long.

From this day until his retirement in 1985, he stood on O'Connell Bridge with a sign around his neck stating 'I Take Photographs'. Gazing through his lens, he'd approach strangers crossing the bridge and would pretend to take their photograph, which would grab their attention and encourage them to stop. At this point, Fields would suggest 'retaking' the photo, just to be on the safe side. This time, he'd actually take the picture, and then he'd give his subjects a ticket so that they could later collect their snapshot from his shop on Pearse Street, where Mrs Fields toiled away in the darkroom. If his customers happened to be in Dublin on holiday, they'd be offered the option of having their souvenir sent to them in the post.

This was his routine every day for over fifty years, as he captured a multitude of Dubliners as they came and went, always walking the three-hour round trip from his home in Raheny to his post on the bridge. Over this time, his style changed very little, apart from when he started using a Polaroid camera in the 1960s, and adopted the catchphrase 'Give it to you now!'

It's estimated that Fields took over 200,000 photographs on that bridge – photographs that are now individually scattered around the world, in family albums, frames, drawers, boxes, attics and sheds. Amongst them are coincidental portraits of celebrities including Brendan Behan, Prince Monolulu, Jack Doyle, Movita Castaneda, Margaret Rutherford, Richard Greene, Noel Purcell and Gene Tierney. In many of his pictures, Nelson's Pillar stands prominently in the background, before abruptly disappearing in 1966. He took photos tracing fads and scenes. He documented Teddy boys, punks, mods and skinheads coming and going. Somewhere out there, there's probably even a photograph of your grandparents on their first date, crossing the bridge on their way to watch a talkie in the Savoy Cinema.

Mary Anne Night-and-Day

Mary Anne Night-and-Day was a little woman who could be seen walking around Grafton Street, Stephen's Green and Harcourt Street. Twenty-four hours a day, seven days a week, she'd make her way around these few blocks at a snail's pace, paying heed to absolutely nobody. She never altered her route or took a diversion, and was therefore equally well known as 'The Circle Woman'.

Mary Ockey

Every day, Mary Ockey – with her cane and her black straw hat – would pop into her local pub on Queen Street, to leave on the bar a little tin can with a handle on the side. Then off she'd go, only to return later on when the barman had kindly filled it with porter for her. She'd attach her newly acquired booze tin to a hook on her belt, cover it with her jacket and walk home a happy woman.

One night, however, one of the drunken barflies heartlessly made a little hole in the can just before Mary showed up to collect her hooch. She secured the tin under her coat as usual, and set off on her commute, only to discover an empty vessel upon her arrival back home. Feeling thoroughly indignant about this treatment, she returned to the pub the next day, fell to her knees and screamed a panoply of curses and insults, fists pumping towards the heavens.

Instead of feeling sorry for her and apologising to her, the culprits started gleefully telling everybody about the mean prank and Mary's consequential breakdown. So from that day on, it became common for the local eejits to jeer at the piteous lady as they cycled past her on the street: 'Mary Ockey, you're an idiot!'

Mary Wallpaper

In a laneway between Newmarket and The Coombe, there sat a car permanently parked and completely covered over with mismatched old wallpaper. Inside the car lived a woman we knew as Mary Wallpaper, for obvious enough reasons. Of course, the thinking behind her exterior decorating was to prevent anybody from seeing inside her home.

Thus, one of the greatest mysteries of Dublin at the time centred around what the interior of that car looked like, and what went on inside the vehicle. As with any great mystery, there emerged plenty of far-fetched theories, making Mary Wallpaper a fearsome and enigmatic figure, exacerbated by the fact that she'd scream and shout at anybody who happened to pass within the vicinity of her car.

For some younger children, it would even be a fear that – in addition to living behind her own wallpaper – Mary was also living behind *their* wallpaper at home, which would result in making bedtime all the more terrifying.

Matt Talbot

Matt Talbot was born in Dublin in 1856, and by the age of 13 was an alcoholic working for a wine merchant.

Over the next few years, alcohol commandeered his life as he spent all of his wages on booze, ran up huge debts, pawned off his clothing, and once even stole a fiddle from a blind street musician to help fund his habit.

Aged 28, Talbot was at his lowest ebb and, unable to procure any booze for himself, took 'The Pledge' (a vow of abstinence conceptualised by Father Theobald Mathew). Over the remaining four decades of his life, Talbot didn't touch a drop of the stuff, instead living his life as though he were a monk in the sixth century. He considered himself to be a slave to the Virgin Mary, attended at least one Mass per day, and could often be seen around town with his head bowed as he rushed from one church to the next.

On 7 June 1924, Talbot was legging it along Granby Lane on the way to Mass when he collapsed and died. At Jervis Street Hospital, doctors discovered the extent of his devotion, noting that his waist, arms and legs were swaddled in flesh-cutting chains and cords. It was also discovered that for decades he had been sleeping on a plank bed with a wooden pillow. Then, for his dinner, he'd boil a herring, feed it to the cat, and then drink the warm fishy water from the pot. The posthumous story of his victory over addiction and his self-flagellating ways made him an inspiration to many, to the point that some Dubliners would pray to him and make offerings in his name.

Patrons of Mr Talbot would also praise the regular donations that he made to the church, although detractors would remark that, on the way to make these donations, he'd be passing by the tenement in which his broke, tuberculosis-ridden sister and her unemployed husband lived. Many of his supporters also admired his good work ethic, whereas his co-workers at the time lamented the fact that he'd volunteer himself to work late, depriving others of what would otherwise be paid overtime.

The writer Brendan Behan claimed that Talbot was despised and ridiculed in his lifetime, and opposed to the pivotal strike of 1913. Seán O'Casey, another playwright and a neighbour of Talbot's, remembered how he'd been dubbed 'Mad Talbot' by those who knew of his ways.

Despite his contemporaneous reputation, in 1975 Pope Paul VI declared him 'Venerable Matt Talbot', the first step in his journey towards becoming a fully fledged saint. Now, in his home town, he has a plaque, a statue and even a bridge. Rehab clinics and recovering alcoholics all over the world claim a debt to him. As if all of that wasn't enough, one episode of the iconic sitcom *Father Ted* mentions a fellow by the name of Matty Hislop, whom Ted describes as 'a notorious drunkard who found God and then decided to punish himself for his sins.'

Whether he was a mentally unstable scab or a miracle worker, Matt Talbot's legacy is legion.

Matt the Jap

In 1979, at the age of 45, Masahiso 'Matteo' Matubara arrived in Dublin to pursue a Master of Letters postgraduate degree in Trinity College. Having already studied in Norway and France, he was extraordinarily well educated by the time he arrived to investigate the links between Arabic and Celtic cultures – and although he was a deaf mute, he was able to understand several languages including Japanese, English, Irish, French, Russian, Norwegian and German.

Despite being awarded his M.Litt in 1987 (with his thesis centred on Islamic journeys in the Middle Ages), he took a liking to Trinity and decided to stick around, becoming a permanent fixture on campus. Well known for his hot temper, generations of students who went along to the university to learn would soon pick up the most important lesson of them all: stay well out of the way of Matt the Jap's walking stick.

In between malevolently knocking over the sign for 'The Buttery' on a daily basis, he maintained a correspondence with some of Europe's most esteemed figures, including Mary McAleese, Cardinal Ratzinger, Jacques Chirac, Prince Charles, Prince Michael and Prince Albert. Despite his friends in high places, he was banned from the college library for desecrating some priceless old manuscripts, including *Táin Bó Cúailnge* – although Matt maintained that he was simply correcting a few typos.

A divisive and eternal presence known variously as 'Matt The Jap', 'Sony' or 'The Japanese Ambassador', it got to the point where it seemed like Matubara would be studying alongside our great-great-grandchildren in many years to come. He was also regularly spotted begging from strangers, availing of the free wine and cheese at assorted functions, and transferring carefully chosen trash from the campus bins into a Dunnes Stores plastic bag.

Thus, it came as an extra surprise when he was found dead in his home on Mount Street in 2007, with around €40,000 cash in his apartment.

Mick McGilligan's daughter, Mary Ann

Not only was this lady's name not Mary Ann, but her father probably wasn't called Mick McGilligan either. She was a banjo-plucking, shawl-wearing lady who could usually be found step-dancing outside William Bushe's pub as she performed 'Mick McGilligan's Daughter, Mary Ann'. This is a risqué old Irish song that assassinates the character and appearance of one Mary Ann McGilligan, albeit in a strangely affectionate way. It was the only tune that our Dorset Street busker knew, so she earned her nickname through countless renditions of a song that contains lyrics like:

> *Sure 'tis aisy to be seen,*
> *That she is no beauty queen,*
> *And her double chin is steamrolled every day.*
> *And her eyebrows they are shifted,*
> *And her face is lifted,*
> *Though who is goin' to lift it, I can't say.*

Bizarrely, Dublin actually had two musicians whose catalogue consisted solely of this song – two Mick Mc Gilligan's Daughter, Mary Anns, if you will. As well as having only one song, the other one had only one leg, and she used to ply her trade on Hanlon's Corner, soliciting whiskey from the farmers who'd be popping out from the cattle market for a pint.

Unfortunately, the writer of this extremely lucrative old song is unknown, so we can never be sure if they picked up the substantial royalties cheque they would have surely been owed by this pair.

Mickey Joe

Mickey Joe was an aul fella who lived in a dairy and never changed his clothes, which consisted of brown trousers, a striped shirt, an open waistcoat and an old cap on his head. Across the arms of his shirt, there'd be big glistening snot patches, which had formed as a result of him attempting to mop up his constantly flowing nose.

Every day, he milked his cows by hand and then took out the horse-and-cart to go and deliver his harvest to the shops. Any discerning milk connoisseurs in The Liberties at the time would've been sure to have kept an eye out for Mickey Joe on his rounds – with his one big, rotten tooth sticking out the front of his mouth – to help deduce which shops were the ones to avoid.

Mickey Joe

Miler

Miler was a meek and quiet lad who wore a grey overcoat that was so long he was nearly tripping over it. He'd busk old classics like 'I'll Take You Home Again, Kathleen' in a hushed, uninspired voice that suggested that he had absolutely no belief in himself as a singer. Whenever he received gratuities from a passer-by, his face would be overcome by a look of genuine surprise that he was actually getting away with this carry-on.

Every Sunday, he'd slowly walk a lap of the Four Courts, whilst still mumbling his way through his repertoire, counting the number of bars in the railings around the grounds of the building. As he went, he'd purposefully touch each one with his forefinger, as if there were nothing in the world more important than ascertaining this elusive figure for once and for all.

To give Miler some closure, in a way, I went and counted them myself. So, dearest Miler, wherever you may be: I want you to know that, excluding gates, I counted exactly 1,794 bars in the railings around the Four Courts.

Molly Malone

Arguably the most famous Dublin 'street character' of all time, Molly Malone is also notable for the fact that she is the only person listed in this book who never actually existed.

In Edinburgh, in 1883, songwriter James Yorkston composed a song that he considered to be a parody of Irish folk songs, complete with mock pathos, gratuitous tragedy and a drunken singalong. The narrative follows a sexy fishmonger, who dies, but returns as a ghost to flog her unsold cockles and mussels. Yorkston chose the name 'Molly Malone' for his protagonist – a supposedly typical Irish name, which happened to fit the cadence perfectly.

A little over a century later, in 1988, the song had become the unofficial anthem of Dublin City, and a statue of the woman was being erected on College Green to celebrate Dublin's 1,000[th] birthday. The wheelbarrow mentioned in the song was substituted for a much classier-looking handcart, but this wasn't the only liberty taken by the city council. Molly's apparent birth and death certificates were unearthed, and we learned that she had lived from 1663 to 1699. June 13th was even declared 'Molly Malone Day', to mark the day of her funeral, in St John's Church on Fishamble Street.

To some people, the statue's low-cut dress and voluptuous figure gave credence to the rumour that Malone's fish-selling was just a front for a prostitution racket – a libellous accusation that isn't, in any way, alluded to in the song's original three verses. The lack of evidence for this idea hasn't prevented the statue from becoming known to

Dubliners as 'The Tart with the Cart', 'The Flirt in the Skirt', 'The Dish with the Fish', 'The Dolly with the Trolley', or the truly desperate 'The Trollop with the Scallops.'

With the made-up lady from his silly little song going on to become one of the most famous people in Dublin's history, perhaps it's fair to credit James Yorkston as the most successful satirical songwriter of all time.

Mullinahack

Mullinahack was a vagabond who matched a flat cap with white runners and went begging from door to door in Dublin, around the time of World War II. He got his name because whenever he received a financial donation, he'd cheerily remark: 'They'll never bate the Chinese out of Mullinahack' – a cryptic and confusing reference to the block just east of John's Lane Church.

So that's where our man got his name from, but Mullinahack itself took its name from the Irish 'Muileann an Chaca', which literally translates as 'mill of excrement'. However, unlike some of our other characters, Mullinahack took no issue with strangers hollering his nickname at him. Perhaps he was unaware of where it had actually came from. It's interesting to note that even the original place itself hadn't been referred to by that name for some years before his time.

Ned Get Up

In the 1930s, one particular gentleman eschewed traditional means of employment and instead spent his weekdays walking from 9 a.m. to 5 p.m.. He'd go down the North Circular Road from Summerhill to Phibsborough, cross the road and walk back again on the other side. It was a round trip that would take the average pedestrian less than an hour, but Ned wasn't the average pedestrian, and his journeys were quite relaxed. He'd even treat himself to a cigarette break whenever he found a used butt on the ground. He did this in a loop. All day. Every day. All whilst muttering to himself – and anyone he passed – the words: 'Get up! Get up! Get up or you'll lose a half!'

Dressed in a huge raincoat, and topped off with a hat with a brim so big that it shadowed most of his face, the only parts of his body even slightly visible were his alert, staring eyes. Somebody seeing Ned for the first time might imagine that he was a top spy or a private detective, covertly patrolling the street and relaying coded messages to a radio transmitter hidden underneath his excessive coat. If only that were the case.

Neighbours in the know knew exactly where Ned's catchphrase came from, and why he haunted the North Circular Road. 'Get up! Get up! Get up or you'll lose a half!' was what Ned's family would yell at him in the morning, back when he had a steady wage and a cushy job – a job that would deduct half a day's wage as punishment for any amount of lateness. As luck would have it, Ned's abysmal punctuality record eventually resulted in him losing this job, and so he became a self-employed creature of habit, endlessly repeating aloud the advice passed down to him from his elders.

So let that be a lesson to you the next time you're having trouble getting out of bed in the morning. Before you roll over to nap for 'just another five minutes,' remember the unfortunate fate of poor Ned Get Up. Surely you don't want to end up like him?

Nittiney Wah Wah

Margaret Bolster was a well-educated lady who came from money, as her father was a chemist with a shop on King Street. She had two houses on Aughrim Street, which she allowed to become dilapidated and dirty over the years, as her own level of personal hygiene plummeted in equal measure. An incredibly quiet and genial lady, she'd often be seen cycling home from the farmers' markets with bales of hay on the back of her bike. When the local kids saw her going by – imaginations fuelled cruelly by the sight of the hay and the whiff off the cyclist – they'd yell out: 'Nittiney Wah Wah has pigs in her kitchen!'

Although this claim transpired to be false, her house was cleared out after she died, and sure enough, the place was packed to the rafters with hay, which she had been using as bedding and which had accumulated over the years, for reasons that must have been personal to poor Ms Bolster.

One Eyeball

One Eyeball was a hairy fellow who lived in The Liberties and got his kicks from scaring the bejaysus out of all the local kids. He'd jump out at children down laneways, blocking their path as he made a loud popping noise with his mouth, slowly removing a marble eye from its gaping socket with his filthy hands. Waving the glistening artefact in their direction, he'd demand that they touch it – of course by this stage the kids would be gone, having sprinted back the way they came.

Because they never stuck around long enough to witness the full spectacle, nobody ever attested to having actually seen One Eyeball's empty socket – which led to some people optimistically suggesting that he was just a lunatic prankster still in possession of both of his original eyes. I ask you! Have you ever heard a more delusional theory? This was obviously just wishful thinking, designed to distract from the sordid reality of a man who brought the terrifying spirit of Japanese legend Tenome to inner-city Dublin.

You'd think that it'd be more than sufficient to have just the one man who went around permanently scarring children with his ocular prosthesis – but One Eyeball wasn't the only Dubliner with a passion for whipping out his eye at inappropriate moments. Yellow Eye Kinsella was fond of performing the exact same stunt in *his* neck of the woods, making sure that the kids of St Theresa's Gardens (off Donore Avenue) were kept on their toes just as much as their peers up the road.

Owny the Fool

Owny was a ginger fellow who went along to every funeral in the city, wearing an ever-decaying black suit. Although he would attend the services of people who he hadn't even met, anybody who was familiar with Owny made sure to stay out of his bad books. Otherwise, he could threaten to skip their inevitable funeral – and what kind of a send-off would it be without Dublin's chief mourner in attendance?

Once, during a service in St Andrew's on Westland Row, a curious pooch wandered up the aisle, interrupting Owny's thoughts and prayers. Without hesitation, Owny did what any good god-fearing man would do and leaped to his feet to give the dog an unmerciful kick, which sent him howling across the church.

Despite his given name (and his questionable treatment of animals), Owny the Fool actually had a reputation for being quite a wise man.

Paddy Carwash

A day patient of St Brendan's Hospital (a Grangegorman-based psychiatric facility), Paddy Carwash would clean your car in exchange for a pint of Guinness. On a profitable day, he'd be walking home absolutely sloshed out of his mind, as half of the cars in Dublin gleamed in the twilight.

Paddy Sugarstick

Charley Donnelly was a lanky fellow who traversed the streets dragging along a cart filled with all sorts of goodies for the kids to play with. An unorthodox type of rag-and-bone man, he'd try to catch the eye of every youngster in Dublin with his attractive crinkled-paper umbrellas, bright, spinning windmills, canal-reed whistles, and a sweetmeat box filled with sugarsticks. It was because of these lollipop-type treats that Donnelly came to be known as 'Paddy Sugarstick', as he'd try to divert people to his little pop-up shop by exclaiming: 'Go and get me an aul jam-jar, or a porter bottle, and I'll give you a big lump o' sugarstick.'

Sugarstick wasn't a jack – or a master – of just one trade, as other days he'd ditch the handcart completely and would sing ballads like 'The Irish Jaunting Car' or 'The Waxies' Dargle' instead. The latter song is a tribute to the cobblers ('waxies') of Dublin, who – unlike the gentry – were unable to afford a holiday by the River Dargle in Wicklow, and thus would organise a budget version just outside the city centre, in Irishtown. In a precursor to the music festivals of today, they'd have picnics with live dance music, and sometimes there'd even be boxing competitions. Treacle Billy would often be plying his trade there too, selling treacle-centred donuts in a tall hat and white coat. When Paddy Sugarstick wasn't flogging homemade children's toys, he'd be doing great justice to this old folk song, and in turn honouring the likes of Treacle Billy. It's only a shame they weren't around at the same time, as you'd imagine that Treacle Billy and Paddy Sugarstick would've gotten along just grand.

This wasn't the extent of Donnelly's talents, though. He was also a fortune-telling organ-grinder who usually set up on Henry Street. On top of his organ sat a cage with two lovebirds imprisoned inside. As he played, passing girls would be encouraged to seek their fortune. Upon crossing Donnelly's palm with silver, he'd open the cage and instruct one of the birds to swoop down into a drawer on the side of the organ, from which it would grab in its beak a piece of paper containing the customer's certain fate. If you wanted to know even more about what the future had in store for you, you could even pick up a copy of *Old Moore's Almanac* from Mr Sugarstick.

On his rare day off, Donnelly would walk with his head bowed, seemingly lost in thought, probably devising his next brilliant enterprise. But he was off-duty, and as far as he was concerned his name had reverted back to being Charley Donnelly. So if you shouted 'Paddy Sugarstick!' at him, you'd want to be ready to run.

Paddy the Liar

*Terrible murdher! Read all about it! Man shoots wife and
all his childer!*

Back in the day, before this type of news story was
just a regular occurrence, such a headline would
be sure to attract people's attention enough for them
to buy a newspaper in order to read the full story. So
Paddy the Liar, a Rathmines-based newspaper vendor,
would use his imagination to the fullest when he needed
to flog a few extra papers. Hoarsely but triumphantly,
he announced fantastical suicides and disasters, which
would prick up the ears of any passers-by. His intentional
yellow journalism puts him in stark contrast to our other
friend, Blind Joe Sadler, who only inadvertently delivered
false stories.

One night on his rounds, old grey Paddy caught a
chill and was taken to hospital. The next day, in amongst
his ramblings to a nurse, he yelled out: 'Evening
Special! The death of Paddy the Liar!' Sure enough, he
passed away that very day, proving that he had been
misunderstood all along. Paddy the Liar was not a liar
after all; he was a seer.

Pat Ingoldsby

In the 1980s, Pat Ingoldsby was a household name and a star of children's television. He was the host of *Pat's Hat*, *Pat's Chat* and *Pat's Pals* on RTÉ, appeared as a storyteller on *Bosco* and wrote a regular column for the *Evening Press*. After controversially reading a poem entitled 'Vagina in the Vatican' on live television, he began to disappear off the radar of the mainstream media – as well as the world of children's TV.

He took to the streets with a pop-up bookshop selling copies of his poetry, plays and stories. Over the years, he could be found on Westmoreland Street, Grafton Street, North Earl Street or Howth Pier, parading his large back-catalogue, which included such titles as 'Welcome to my Head (Please Remove Your Boots)', 'You've Just Finished Reading this Title' and 'I Thought You Died Years Ago'. Into all of his books, the notoriously anti-establishment fellow inserts an ingenious invented clause, which allegedly prevents them from being used in school textbooks, exams, elocution classes or 'anything with the word "Arts" in it.'

In 1893, W. B. Yeats referred to Zozimus as 'the last of the gleemen,' but he obviously failed to foresee the coming of Pat Ingoldsby – an old-fashioned travelling bard to rival the best of them. Alongside his life's work, Pat always has a few cheeky handmade signs to attract the attention of passing tourists – although it would take a brave one to photograph him or these signs without expressing any actual interest in making a purchase...

Pat Ingoldsby

Peggy Leg

According to various European folktales, the Devil has the very cool ability to take on any human form he desires – be it a little old lady or a charming young prince. Whilst using this dark magic, he must always keep one cloven hoof on display, as a warning to humankind that evil lurks. In a further bout of devilment, he'd sometimes try to disguise the hoof as something like a wooden leg or a club foot, so as not to give the game away too early. It always helps to go incognito when you're the Devil.

This terrifying thought brings us to The Liberties, where an unfortunate lady with a club foot was known locally as 'Peggy Leg'. As if that wasn't bad enough, her well-dressed husband sent her out begging every day – even while she was pregnant – dressed in tattered children's clothes. But wait: there's more.

To top off Peggy Leg's list of woes, many of the local children considered her to be Lucifer himself. They thought that Satan had returned to the world in inner-city Dublin, as the miserable, abused wife of some scummy blaggard. Naturally, Peggy was feared by all the little kids, who stayed well away from her. Then they grew up, became terrible teens, got a bit bolder, and would taunt her whenever they were feeling mean, screaming 'Peggy Leg, Peggy Leg' as she hobbled sadly down the street.

Plush Maggie

Plush Maggie was a tall, thin lady who wore a red plush cape which almost covered her entire frame. She lived off scraps – wherever she could find them – and whenever she saw people eating, she'd try to put them off finishing their food so that she might be able to tuck in instead.

Nobody was safe, and neither were any of the food groups. You could be daydreaming on your lunch break, munching a sandwich as you watch the ducks in the park. You could be chewing on an apple at the bus stop, desperate to get home after a long day at work. You could be demolishing a large popcorn at the cinema, enthralled by the action on the big screen.

Then suddenly you'd hear the discouraging words of Plush Maggie forming in the ether: 'You're not going to finish that… go on, throw it away… you don't want it… why would you want to eat that… throw it away…'.

Pound Note

Pound Note greatly resembled a morbidly obese man, but this wasn't the case. All of that excess weight came from the fact that his clothes were stuffed full of countless bits of paper that he had crammed into his pockets, down his sleeves and into the lining.

Once upon a time, he had found a pound note on the ground, and from that day on he never walked past a stray piece of paper on the street. When he came across something of interest, he craned his neck to see if there was anybody watching, pounced on it as soon as the coast was clear, and then shoved it into his coat.

As is the case with any growing business enterprise, Pound Note's wastepaper collection demanded a bigger working space over time. So, as his venture expanded, so did his clothes, with additional pockets being sewn into his coat. This still wasn't enough, and soon Pound Note was also seen to be dragging around a couple of teeming sacks over his shoulders. He never examined his findings until he got back to his headquarters on Eccles Street, so it's not public knowledge whether or not he ever again tasted the glory of that fateful day on which he found free money on the street.

Pound Note

President Keely

Terence Keely was a short fellow with a mane of white hair down to his shoulders. Atop his head was a tall silk hat with his name emblazoned upon it. He also had the voice of a lion – to match his mane – which he used to speak up for those who had none.

During each and every election campaign, posters promoting Fianna Fáil and Cumann na nGael would be plastered over every square inch of free space around the city. In amongst these were charming DIY notices, chalked or painted on the wall, advertising the candidacy of one self-styled 'President Keely'. Alongside the platitudes of the running parties were Keely's infinitely more inspiring slogans, like 'The ship can't go out if it doesn't come in' and 'The sun will never fall in Dublin… it'll do as I say.'

Keely's Dublin was one that was still in tatters after the Civil War, so any political discussion tended to be a heated affair, often descending into violence. In stark contrast, his presence provided some balance and offered the people much-needed relief from the 'real' issues of the day. Whilst the establishment discussed serious business at the grown-ups' table, Keely's sideshow instead focused on pledges like providing boots for the barefoot children of Dublin, or disapproving of the brazen slack-wearing ladies of the city who had been overly inspired by Jean Harlow in Howard Hughes's 1930 blockbuster *Hell's Angels*. They all needed to pay a visit to their local chapel to be exorcised, according to Keely.

Writer Lar Redmond remembered one particular day, when one national hero was outside the GPO sharing his ideas for the improvement of the Irish Free State. Unfortunately, he had some competition standing on top of an orange box at the corner of Abbey Street, where Keely was declaring his own plans for the betterment of the country – plans that our 'real' politician could only dream about. The first order of business would be to turn the south-facing Nelson's Pillar around so that it was looking north instead, because that womaniser Horatio Nelson had absolutely no right to be looking down on our beloved Daniel O'Connell. After that, new legislation would be passed to grant all unemployed people 'jobs with twelve months holidays, and all but one week with double pay.'

As he spoke, some youngsters who had climbed up a lamp post started slagging him, so Keely went on a diatribe against the new generation, which he believed had no respect for their elders. This inspired him to take his speech in a new direction, as he promised to open up more reformatories for the youth, telling his detractors up the lamp post that 'if this was Russia, yiz'd be thrun' into the Liffey.' It wasn't long before the entire rally had shifted themselves away from the GPO to listen to Keely instead, as he seemed to be entertaining his crowd considerably more than whoever it was outside the post office. Keely's congregation expanded to the point that the Gardaí had to move in to break things up, as our president protested about being censored and exclaimed that he had a right to freedom of speech and expression.

Despite his truly unique philosophies, and the overwhelming amount of public support he received, President Keely never managed to make it as far as Áras an Uachtaráin. He lived to see Douglas Hyde and Seán O'Kelly make their home in the Phoenix Park, before trading the Liffey for the Mersey to be with his daughters, who had married Englishmen. In Birkenhead, he retired from his political career for good and became one of *their* local characters instead, as he went around the pubs playing the pennywhistle in his top hat.

President Keely died in 1953. Sadly, he was the only president in history to be sent off without the dignity of a formal state funeral.

Razorblades

This fellow used to hang around outside a shop near Christchurch, with one of his hands permanently hovering inside of his coat. Naturally, this extremely suspicious loitering led to much speculation about the nature of his business. One of the most often touted ideas was that he was concealing some sort of weapon – potentially some form of knife. Plenty of kids would say, 'Howaya, Razorblades' as they walked by him, but then they'd pick up the pace because of course Razorblades did not like being called that. Perhaps he knew that the kids were on to him.

Red Fitz

A native of Kevin Street, Red Fitz could be seen in the area – and heard even farther afield – covered in red paper from top to tail, and beating and whistling a military march. He alternated between playing a melodeon and using a big tin can for percussion, which he hung from his waist as he stepped in a perfectly regimented fashion.

The fact that he was able to perform such a convincing impersonation of a soldier is probably because he had once been one. Another name we had for Red Fitz was 'The Bombay Deserter', as rumour had it that he had ditched his army unit – stationed in India – to return to Dublin and, assumedly, follow his true calling for ever more.

Shellshock Joe

Another one of our former soldiers, Shellshock Joe used to go ballistic at the sight of Kevin Street police station. Unfortunately, he had a tendency to pass it almost every day. To some people, it even seemed like he might have been going out of his way to catch a glimpse of it. Any excuse for a tantrum!

As soon as he saw the building, his fury overtook his sense of reason. He'd run into the middle of the road to launch his attack, ignoring all of the cars on the road, as well as the vexed and cursing drivers behind the steering wheels. Standing militantly on the cobbles, he'd bite imaginary pins out of imaginary grenades and he'd lob them straight in through the entrance doors of the station.

Joe would always continue to unleash his imaginary carnage upon the building and the occupants within, until a patient guard came along to subdue him and lead him away. With Kevin Street station out of sight and out of mind, Joe would become placid again… until the next time. In his mind, the battle was over, but the war was still raging.

Sikey

In the early twentieth century, a tall, athletic man stood atop a shiny black box in Dublin city centre, advertising Nugget boot polish. It was the best advertising any company could possibly hope for, because this man was one of the first ever black people to live in what might be the world's palest country, and was thus guaranteed to attract attention from any passers-by.

The son of a slave, 'Cyclone' Billy Warren was a Boston-born boxer who earned his stripes fighting in battles royal, where four African-American fighters were blindfolded and put into a ring to bare-knuckle box each other. The last man standing took the prize – a purse that usually contained a fairly petty sum.

Billy ended up living in Europe at the turn of the century, participating in fights across the UK, France and Ireland. He was even crowned Irish Heavyweight Champion in 1909, after beating Jem Roche in Belfast in one of his few recorded victories. The legitimacy of this title was later disputed because of the fact that Warren wasn't actually Irish. Conspiracy theorists on his side, Roche claimed the title in a repeat bout the following month.

Warren married a lady from Wolverhampton, but racism was rife in post-war England, and a black pugilist had little chance of getting work – with even less chance of finding accommodation if he was successful in booking a fight. So the couple decided to move to famously friendly Dublin, and into No. 32 Nelson Street on the north side of the river.

Back then, seeing a person of colour in Dublin was a complete novelty, and The Cyclone (or 'Sikey' as he was renamed by the locals) thrived as a nine days' wonder, strutting around the city wearing a bowler hat and a Crombie coat, with a fancy cravat and a carnation in the lapel. Bearing in mind that he was also a former heavyweight champion, some smaller children would shy away from him or cross the road when they saw him coming. Sikey humoured these scaredy-cats by pretending to chase them, waving his cane and barking 'Grrrr... me big black man, eat white people!'

The rest of the locals thought that he was a fantastic character and they'd all hang around with him outside of the GPO listening to all of his wild stories. Boxing and promoting shoe polish weren't his only jobs though: he also played the part of a slave in an epic 1920 silent movie entitled *In the Days of Saint Patrick*. The level of affection shown towards Sikey is probably best represented by Sir William Orpen's painting *The Winner (The Champ)'* – a portrait of the boxer victoriously raising a gloved fist. Warren died in 1951 and is buried in Mount Jerome Cemetery.

Slep' with the Nuns

In 1940s Dublin – back when there were no gagging orders, superinjunctions or defamation suits – we had an old lad called Slep' with the Nuns who lived around Blackhorse Lane (now Blackhorse Avenue). Mystery shrouds the circumstances of how he came to be bestowed with this somewhat embarrassing moniker, but we do know that he definitely didn't embrace it.

He'd be cycling home through Stoneybatter on his way back from town, minding his own business, when a gang of kids would yell his nickname at him. In response, Slep' with the Nuns would have a full-on breakdown, throwing down his bike and standing in the middle of the road screaming furiously and unintelligibly. There are two theories as to what it was that he was shouting about: he was either trying to figure out where this vicious rumour had come from, or else he was cursing the day that he ever set foot in that convent.

Slim

In a time before internet streaming, torrents and pirated DVDs, if you didn't have the money for a cinema ticket, you'd be left with no option but to miss out on the latest blockbuster to hit Dublin's theatres. So it was just as well that this fellow named Slim existed.

He'd go to every movie that was released, and then, after the end credits, he'd find a secluded environment. It was here that people would gather to hear him re-enact the entire film, from start to finish. He'd play every character, describe every scene, hum the music and recreate the sound effects, immersing everybody in all of the action. It got to the point where it wasn't just the penniless who'd sit listening, wide-eyed with attention, because Slim's dramatisations were often considered to be even better than the real thing.

Soodlum

There was a guy called Mr Healy, better known as 'Soodlum', who was a quaint little fellow with a scruffy moustache on his rounded red face. He was always moving from one lodging house to another – to the extent that it was said that he had never slept in the same bed twice. He also had a reputation for approaching young women on the street and asking them 'Will I take it out for you, Miss?' These ladies would usually take off down the street for fear of what 'it' might be. This was their own loss, though, as Healy (a talented musician) was only ever planning on whipping out his tin whistle to woo them with a tune.

As a rag-and-bone man, he was used to lugging around a heavy sack filled with all sorts of odds and ends. Even when he was off duty, he'd walk around with his left hand across his chest, still transporting his phantom swag. All the while, he sang in a rumbling voice:

> *Watchin' the mill go rounda,*
> *Oh watchin' the mill go rounda,*
> *I loved her because she was poora.*
> *It broke the heart of Mary Jane,*
> *Watchin' the mill go rounda.*

Once a week, he headed over to the barracks on Ship Street. Coincidentally enough, he always seemed to stop by on the soldiers' payday. He stood on the middle of the road singing his song, serenading the troops at their windows. They made it a game to think up new pranks to play on him every month. One particular favourite was to throw down hot pennies at his feet. Soodlum knew exactly what they wanted, and he wasn't going to disappoint them. After all, a hot penny was still a penny – once it had cooled down, at least.

He'd pick up one of the pennies, feign pain and spit profanities whilst blowing his supposedly burnt fingers. The soldiers would of course crack up laughing at these ridiculous antics. Then Soodlum would act as though he was reverting to Plan B, gathering all the pennies into a pile using the toe of his boot. All the while, he'd be keeping a close eye on his growing mound of change and throwing dirty looks at the nearby children, a pack of whom would be greedily eyeing up his hard-earned cash.

Before departing, he'd chance his arm one last time. He'd hold up one of his ammunition boots for reference, and say to his benefactors: 'have ye any ol' pairs of amms?' The good soldiers, noticing his dilapidated footwear, would usually find it in their hearts to throw him down a few boots that were just lying around up there. Of course, the next time Soodlum paid them a visit, he'd be wearing the same broken boots that he'd arrived in the last time.

Based on this little charade, it's likely that, when he died in 1930, so did the black market for ammunition boots in Dublin.

Stack of Rags

As was the case with anybody sent to the House of Industry, Stack of Rags was an unsightly and unprofitable drifter whom the government wished to keep off the streets of Dublin. His name came from the ludicrous amount of swaddling in which he insulated himself, which made him look more like a big ol' pile of clothes than a human being.

Soon after his incarceration in 1816, he began to provoke suspicion when the workers noticed how little his attire changed in a warmer indoor environment, and the peculiar way that he acted whenever he was approached by anybody.

When they finally got around to inspecting this gentleman a little bit more closely, it was discovered that he had over seventy-five guineas in gold sewn into his rags, and bank receipts for several lodgements he had made, amounting to £1,500 in total.

Stoney Pockets

An acquaintance of Zozimus, Stoney Pockets was born with a postural disability that tilted his body to one side. His mother's cure for this affliction was to weigh down one of his pockets with rocks and stones, forcing him to stand up straight and, in his own words, to 'keep me head from flyin' away.' His obituary from May 1840 refers to him as 'a miserable, low-sized, half-naked ragged individual who was generally followed by a crowd of little boys.' They certainly didn't beat around the bush back in those days.

Swing

Swing was a tall, pale busker with a big black beard, greasy mackintosh coat and a cloth cap atop his head. Despite his blindness, he was a maestro at the tin whistle and his talent probably could've earned him quite a few bob, were it not for the fact that he had a slightly limited repertoire. However, it is apparent that, throughout time, plenty of other street musicians have managed to scrape together a living despite only knowing one or two songs – so why was Swing so unfortunate in this regard? Well, it might be because the only tune that Swing could play was a famous old number entitled 'God Save the Queen.'

He got his name because, as he walked the streets, hecklers would dare him by saying 'Swing, you devil, swing.' He'd respond to this by agitatedly swirling in a circle, swinging his walking stick around in the air, hoping that it'd meet with one of his tormentors. By that stage, they'd be long gone and poor Swing would end up whacking some poor innocent bystander.

Perhaps Swing had just awoken from a long slumber. Perhaps his lack of vision meant that he was unable to read the newspapers, or the history books, and was thus unaware that certain events had occurred. Perhaps he was a staunch Unionist, bravely airing his allegiances in an independent Ireland. Whatever the reason, he definitely would've been better off airing his *feadóg* virtuosity somewhere like Bethnal Green instead of Stephen's Green.

Tiddle the Stars

Tiddle the Stars stood out in the middle of the road at night, with his head craned back, pointing at the sky and wiggling his fingers around like a baby playing with an invisible mobile hung over its cot with invisible string.

To anybody watching, it looked as though he was trying to tickle the stars – a romantic yet impossible notion, which may have been a consequence of his alleged shellshock (this was the mid twentieth century, after all). Of course, in Ireland, there's a tendency to refer to tickling as 'tiddling', and so that is how he got his name.

Tiddle The Stars is not to be confused with one-time Harold's Cross native 'Tiddle The Bricks' – a man who walked along the footpath in such close proximity to the wall that he was practically tickling its bricks.

Tiddle the Stars

Tie-Me-Up

Tie-Me-Up's routine was to stand topless beside the Ha'penny Bridge, cracking a whip and yelling 'Tie me up. Tie me up!' Then he'd get a couple of men to bind him in chains and put him into a straitjacket, at which point he would attempt to free himself from his shackles, as the crowd around him grew bigger and bigger.

Dozens of entranced onlookers watched nervously as he rolled, spun and jerked around on the pavement whilst screaming like a banshee, with his eyes fit to burst out of their sockets. Around ten minutes later, Tie-Me-Up would step out of his restraints and bow to his adoring audience. Let me tell you one thing: that Houdini fella had nothing on ol' Tie-Me-Up.

But the show wasn't over yet! For his encore, Tie-Me-Up would perform one of his other weird tricks, like bending a six-inch-long nail, ripping up a phone book, or lying down on a load of broken glass for the craic.

On a lucky Saturday afternoon, you'd be able to catch a few other performers at work by the bridge, including Blondini (a sword swallower), The Cartwheel Man (a guy who was able to balance a cartwheel on his chin, like a sea-lion with a red ball on its nose) and The Whip Man (Dublin's answer to William Tell – a fellow known for his ability to deftly whip cigarettes out of his wife's mouth).

Tom the Doll Man

When Tom the Doll Man rolled onto your street, he'd unpack a large wooden box on the kerb. Then out would come two brightly dressed life-size dolls, which Tom would mount on a board on top of the box. He'd sit down beside them and start playing the mouth organ with one hand, as his other hand connected to wires that were attached to the figures.

As soon as the dolls heard his spirited harmonica playing, they would both come to life with a merry jig. As the dolls' legs moved in time with the music, it really gave the appearance that Tom was a magic man who had them under his spell, and the locals would all gather around to marvel at his wizardry.

Tom the Moon

Tom the Moon was a shabbily dressed aul fella who'd have a permanent grin on his face as he sang old ballads for money. But nobody was interested in hearing him sing. As he performed, kids would skip and hop around him, drowning out his dulcet tones with screeches of 'Oh, Tom! Tom! Show us the moon!'

They didn't have to wait long, because after each song Tom would take off his grubby cap, hopefully to collect a few coins.

And there it was.

The moon. The full moon, in all its resplendent glory, shining, hairless and greasy, complete with craters and all.

Our amateur astronomers would squeal with delight at the sight of Tom's big baldy head, and their admiration would make The Moon glow even more than usual.

Tom the Moon

Tom Tutty

Tom Tutty was a remnant of the Teddy boy scene, from the early days of rock and roll. He used to live in an iron shed underneath a footbridge in Cowper, but took to wandering the streets when the bridge was demolished in the 1980s. Because it isn't possible to receive benefits with no fixed abode, and he was entitled to an army pension, his address was registered with the state as Jack Birchall's pub in Ranelagh.

His calling card was an extra-long ring of the doorbell, which would be the resident's cue to go and fill up his empty glass bottle with some milky tea. This tea would then act as a fuel for his public dance parties, as he'd frolic down the middle of the street, blaring music from a ghetto blaster on his shoulder. He was like the Pied Piper with the ladies, as he'd always end up accumulating a few women who'd join in the parade and pull some moves as they followed him down the street.

Of course, Tutty's procession would always lead to a bumper-to-bumper traffic jam filled with fuming drivers, but he'd be blasting his Tina Turner tape so loud that he wouldn't even be able to hear their irate beeps.

Tom Tutty

Tommy Atkins

Tommy Atkins was a thoroughly kempt man, with grey whiskers and an overcoat, which he wore whatever the weather. He stood on Bride Street singing 'Private Tommy Atkins' by Henry Hamilton, which is how he acquired his pseudonym. The song centres around the fact that, back in the nineteenth century, 'Tommy Atkins' was a generic name used on British War Office forms, and thus it became a term used to refer to British soldiers.

> *Tommy, Tommy Atkins*
> *You're a 'good un', heart and hand,*
> *You're a credit to your calling,*
> *And to all your native land;*
> *May your luck be never failing,*
> *May your love be ever true!*
> *God bless you, Tommy Atkins,*
> *Here's your country's love to you!*

The Irish Tommy Atkins even had a big, knobbled walking stick, which he'd flamboyantly wave around in the air during the chorus, as if he were conducting a full orchestra. Another one of his favourites was 'The Real Irish Stew', which discusses the merits of one of our national dishes and heartily dismisses the cuisine of several other nations, before repeatedly arriving to the triumphant conclusion:

Hurrah for an Irish stew,
That will stick to your belly like glue –
The sons of St Patrick forever,
And three cheers for a real Irish stew!

The Toucher Doyle

The Toucher Doyle was a Machiavellian chancer with a wizened face and pointy ears who lived on Hendrick Street. Despite his elf-like appearance – or perhaps because of it – he managed to find himself in the front line of photographs of every major event that took place, alongside significantly more important people. Most of these events were race meetings, and Doyle's social standing noticeably improved when – after a successful day out betting – he'd buy a round of drinks for the gang in St John's pub on Queen Street.

He even got his name at one of these races, when he went down to the Curragh and typically ended up schmoozing with a visiting King Edward VII. Doyle apparently offered the monarch a fiver if he'd let him touch him, and from that day forth he was known as The Toucher Doyle.

The Toucher has been immortalised in a number of ways. First of all, he gets a mention in the first draft of

James Joyce's *Finnegans Wake*. His next appearance was in
Harry Kernoff's 1948 oil painting *A Bird Never Flew on One
Wing*, which depicts Doyle – cigarette behind his ear and
pint in his hand – boozing with Dublin's Lord Mayor, Alfie
Byrne. For decades, this painting hung in O'Brien's pub on
Leeson Street, until it was sold for €180,000 in 2008.

The most interesting of Doyle's deifications is the
theory that somebody involved in the making of *Star
Trek* was drinking in O'Brien's at some point, saw the
painting, and based the appearance of Mister Spock on
The Toucher Doyle. This premise must have some veracity
– how else could a space alien from a far-off planet have
ended up with the same distinctive ears, hair, eyebrows and
cheekbones as The Toucher Doyle from Smithfield?

The Toucher Doyle

Ubi Dwyer

In the 1980s, shoppers on Grafton Street were likely to bump into a bearded man handing out pro-marijuana flyers and flogging copies of the anarchist newspaper *Freedom*, dressed in a priest's cassock and with a matching zucchetto atop his head. This was William Ubique Dwyer, a man who was as likely to be seen donning a hippie poncho and a floppy hat, with an oversized yellow smiley face stitched to each article of clothing. He was a free-thinking, anti-establishment figure who referred to authority as 'the forces of awe and boredom' and whose ultimate objective was to give Queen Elizabeth II 'the great heave-ho!'

Ubi was born in 1933 and emigrated down under whilst in his twenties, making a name for himself in New Zealand as part of the anarchist movement of the swinging sixties. He got into a little bit of trouble with the law – once for selling acid and once for calling his old friend the Queen 'a bludger' in a public speech – and was deported from Australia in 1969. In the previous century, around 40,000 criminals had been sent on prison ships from Ireland to Oz; now the tables had been turned and Ubi was forced to return to his own hemisphere.

Along with a gang of his hippie cronies, he took up residence on the Merrion Road in posh Ballsbridge, squatting in a vacant house and forming the well-known 'Island Commune'. Unfortunately, this idyllic rent-free retreat for disenfranchised youngsters had to be later abandoned when one mentally disturbed resident attempted to poison everybody in the house. Ubi's reputation was such that he was apparently headhunted by John Lennon to help himself and Yoko Ono to establish a commune of their own on Dorinish, a tiny island off the coast of Mayo that they had purchased for £1,700. Instead, he decamped to London, leaving Sid Rawle ('The King of the Hippies') to work with John and Yoko on the (eventually scrapped) project.

Dwyer took up work as a civil servant in London, where his arch-enemy became his boss at Her Majesty's Stationery Office – but he still found a way to rebel, and always made liberal use of the office facilities to print out anti-monarchist literature. In August 1972, he spearheaded the first of three instalments of the Windsor Free Festival, a seminal social gathering that, true to form, took place in the Queen's back garden, aka Windsor Great Park. These events argued against the archaic feudal system of rent-paying, and marked a pivotal moment in the history of British counter-culture. The police eventually called a halt to the concert series by putting barbed wire around the site and flooding the park with sewage.

Later that decade, Ubi returned to Dublin and in August 1978 he put together another of his free gigs, to be held at the bandstand in The Hollow in the Phoenix Park – groups such as Clannad, Horslips, Paul Brady and U2 were amongst those lined up to play at the three-day Free Peace Festival. A few hours into the first day's proceedings, Ubi drunkenly wandered off-site and made his way to Dún Laoghaire ferry port. The event was a sparsely attended washout that had none of the revolutionary spirit of its London counterpart, and a few days later Ubi was arrested by Thames Valley Police on his way into Windsor Park, hoping to revive his original concept.

Back in Dublin, he moved into a caravan in the back garden of his mother's house in Glenageary. This also became the headquarters for his political campaign when Ubi ran for a seat in Dáil Éireann in 1981 and 1982 with his one-man 'Justice Party'. His election posters featured slogans like 'Vote for the Justice Party and See What Happens', alongside photographs of his bright-yellow bicycle, which he called Senator Sunflower. Despite receiving nearly 1,000 votes from forward-thinking citizens, neither Ubi Dwyer nor Senator Sunflower were ever elected to parliament.

The Window Pest

The Kildare Street Club existed between the years of 1782 and 1977. It was a sort of gentleman's club with close ties to the Protestant Ascendancy and Irish Unionism. Inside the building, members played billiards and cards as they snacked on oysters and caviar. In a poverty-stricken Ireland, these people made up what we might refer to today as 'the top 1 per cent.' Anybody who walked along the street outside the club would be greeted by quite a sight in the window – a creepy silhouetted form who resembled a figurehead of all the selfish debauchery that went on inside.

This shape belonged to a man named Paginini, who sat inside the window of the club for a couple of decades, permanently glaring out on to Stephen's Green. His head had been twisted in some bizarre hunting accident, which meant that his neck had drooped down to rest on his shoulder. Looking down upon the common people from the window seat of this odious, aristocratic establishment, Paginini gave so many citizens so many frights that he came to be known as 'The Window Pest'.

The Window Pest

Zozimus

Michael Moran was born on Faddle's Alley, between Clanbrassil Street and Blackpitts, in 1794. He lost the sight in both of his eyes at only a few weeks old, and was sent out to beg as a boy. In a poverty-stricken Dublin filled with competitive beggars, his blindness almost came as an advantage to him and his family as it made him more deserving of charity than many of his peers. A further advantage came as Moran grew older and discovered some of his talents, like his phenomenal memory and his thunderous voice. So, for the majority of his life, he was able to rely more on his abilities instead of his disability, singing ballads and reciting poetry on bridges and street corners.

He became known to the people of Dublin as 'Zozimus', which was a bastardisation of the name of Saint Zosimas of Palestine, a key character in one of Moran's most popular poems. This glum yet oft-requested epic was his own version of Bishop Anthony Coyle's poetic adaptation of the story of the sinful Mary of Egypt, who was eventually redeemed by the monk Zosimas.

Every day, our Zoz would be guided to one of his posts by his loyal companion Stoney Pockets. After asking his buddy: 'Am I in the right place? I'm not in a puddle, am I?', he'd introduce himself to the crowd and the show would begin:

Ye sons and daughters of Erin!
Gather 'round poor Zozimus, yer friend.
Listen boys, until yiz hear,
My charming song so dear.

Then out would come the aforementioned story of Saint Mary, something like: 'St Patrick Was a Gentleman', or else one of his own compositions, such as 'The Twang Man' (a poem about a toffee salesman driven to murder his love rival), 'Ye Men of Sweet Liberties Hall' (a pro-Home Rule love song to the Liberties), 'The Finding of Moses' (an irreverent re-enactment of the day Moses was found in the rushes), 'Billy's Downfall' (Moran's sworn affidavit that he had no involvement in the bombing of College Green's William of Orange statue), 'Dicky in the Yeomen' (a diss poem, disparaging a member of the Yeomanry), 'Maguire's Triumph' (an ode to Father Thomas Maguire, who won a controversial debate with a Protestant Reverend in 1827), or 'In Praise of Poteen' (you can probably guess the subject matter of this one).

In his cape, ankle-length frieze coat, brown beaver hat, corduroy trousers and Francis Street brogues, and with his blackthorn stick strapped to his wrist, Zozimus could be found performing anywhere from the Smithfield market to the Donnybrook Fair. One report from the fair sees our hero referred to as 'a womanish man… breakfasting on beef as hard as leather or porter as muddy as puddle.'

Once, on Carlisle (now O'Connell) Bridge, a passer-by offered him a generous sixpence if he could rhyme something with the word 'bridge'. With great conviction, Zoz won the bet by immediately bellowing:

> *Ah, kind Christian, do not grudge,*
> *The sixpence promised on the bridge!*

His recitals were liable to attract so many spectators that he frequently ran into trouble with the law, and sometimes ended up in court a few times a year. On one such occasion, accused of 'obstruction and annoyance', he responded to the charges by preaching:

> *Your Worship, what I sing is the praises of*
> *me native land.*
> *I love me country. She's dear to me heart.*
> *Am I to be prevented from writin'*
> *songs in her honour?*
> *It is true that I can't see, but I can warble that which can*
> *rise the heart of me countrymen.*
> *And if crowds gather 'round me, how can I help it?*

Prior to his death on 3 April 1846, Zozimus began to develop a deep fear of ending up under a scalpel at The College of Surgeons courtesy of the infamous body-snatchers, so Stoney Pockets collected enough money for him to be buried within the safe confines of Glasnevin Cemetery. As Stoney later remarked, it was probably for the best that they kept him out of reach of the sack-em-ups, or else the results of Moran's post-mortem examination might have led to whiskey being prohibited forever.

Not long after his death at No. 14 Patrick Street, an imposter showed up in the pubs around the area, dressed like Zozimus, acting like him, and claiming to be him. He hoped to move in on the receiving end of all of the free whiskey droppings that were usually reserved for ol' Zoz, but of course the barmen knew to show him the door. Zozimus lived on through more than just doppelganger con artists, though, as he is remembered as 'The Blind Bard of The Liberties' and 'The Last Gleeman of the Pale', with William Butler Yeats even describing him as 'a poet jester and newsman of the people.'

184B

In the Irish countryside, the police force had their hands full, keeping down illegal poteen rings and repressing faction fighting. At this time there was a lot less criminality in the city, so Dublin-based officers kept themselves busy by going after beggars and street artists. Dublin Metropolitan Police Constable 184B seemed to have a particular dislike for ballad singers and poets, so poor ol' Zozimus was top of his hit list, and he would interrupt his performances and move him on at every possible opportunity.

At this stage, Zozimus had more than earned the respect of his fellow Dubliners and had been an inspiration to many of his contemporaries. So, understandably, 184B's antics got the goat of a slew of people, including some journalists from the *Freeman's Journal*, whose feathers he had also ruffled. In retaliation, all of the disgruntled hacks and street entertainers teamed together regularly to lampoon him in newspaper articles and song, including Zozimus's '184B', which features the line:

> *If I could see this bob,*
> *I'd take my stick this way,*
> *An' be the powers, I'd break his gob.*

184B soon became a laughing stock. Even tourists to Dublin would treat him as their main attraction, going out of their way to find him so that they could follow him around in a pack, hurling abuse at him and laughing at his every move.

He became a liability to the police force and ended up being removed from his position. They even had to take his number out of circulation for years, because no policeman in his right mind would ever want to be seen on the beat wearing a vest that identified him as the infamous 184B. And by god, I bet that fellow never bothered another busker for as long as he lived – plain proof that the pen is indeed mightier than the sword, and that the human voice is even mightier again.

Epilogue

M any of Dublin's beloved street characters were known by and are remembered only by the name that was imposed upon them by their community, rather than the one bestowed upon them by their family. As this book has shown, entire lives of thought, emotion, laughter, love, tragedy, work, education, imagination and conversation were distilled into short, snappy nicknames like Hairy Lemon, The Dead Man or Jembo No-Toes.

Whether they like it or not, we can deduce a lot about a stranger from their nickname, and we can imagine a whole lot more. Across the world, many monikers are designated based on a person's physical appearance (hence generic pseudonyms like 'Fatso', 'Ginger' and 'Smiley'), but in Dublin we have had so many fantastically named citizens that it would be a shame to leave out some of them – the likes of Fr. Flash Kavanagh (so called because he gave the quickest Mass in Dublin – a Latin service clocking in at around twelve minutes), Fish (a petty criminal who always got away from the guards by abruptly leaping into the River Liffey and disappearing), Mary Ate the Flays (a woman who somehow looked like she ate fleas), Polio Bingo (a polio-afflicted man who sold bingo cards door-to-door) and Billy 'The Back of the Neck' Delaney (a milk-seller in the habit of slapping the back of his neck and screaming 'the back of the neck!').

So here, for your perusal, or if you're ever stuck for baby names, is another gang of idiosyncratic individuals who have brightened up Dublin's streets throughout the ages. From their names alone, perhaps you can conjure up your own sense of who they were and/or where they got their name from. Who knows… if you've ever spent a bit of time in Dublin yourself, maybe one of these people is actually *you,* but you're just too blissfully ignorant to realise what people call you behind your back. Perhaps your own bizarre quirks – and some of the mad things that you get up to – don't go completely unnoticed after all….

Bah Furlong
Ballyshannon
The Baltic Brothers
The Bare Wall
The Blind Artillery Man
Bluebeard
Bobby Capper
Brien O'Brien
Bubble Ear
Bucket up the Wall
Burlington Bertie
The Burned Sailor
Cappo
Captain Debrisay
Captain von Sausage
Chase the Hearse
Christy Sweets
Chucky Hayes and Tall Hayes
Cockle-Large-Cock
Davy Stephens
Dan the Ragman

Doctor Duberry
The Dredger
Drummer Maher
Dunlavin
Dynamite
The Earl of Dalgashin
The Earl of Mustard
Fat Mary
Felix the Barber
Flea Picker
Gather-Em-Up
Gorilla Woman
The Grand Old Man
Greenteeth Kelly
The Grindstone Man
Happy Moments
Head in the Pot
Irish Nanny
Jack the Rag
Javey Fennelly
Jose Reynolds
Joseph Damer
Joxer Moore
The Judge
Kate Strong
Kearney the Singer
Keg the Man
The Lavender Man
The Lavender Woman
Mad Essie
Mad Mick
Mad Nelly

The Major
Mary Banger
Michael Bruen
Mickser Reid
Nancy Needleballs
Old Damn
Old Nosey
The Oyster Man
Paddy Alright
Paddy Cummins
Paddy Drac
Pally White
Peg the Man
Penny's the Song
Pete Not-So-Short
Pig's Eye
The Pig Man
The Pocket
Pom-Pom
The Professor
Red Pole Welsh
Robin Hood
Rusty Razors
Scutterbullet
Shakey Shannon
Sissy Look-Up
Skin the Goat
The Slopman
Specs
Springheel Jack
The Spudneck King
Stab the Rasher

Stop, Stand and Stare
Steevens
Take Down the Bed
Tom Troy
The Tuggers
Turkey Hole
Two Thumps
The Umbrella Man
Watercress
Watty Cox
Weep Weep
Windy Mills
The Woman with the Pig's Head
The Yank Mooney
The Yupper